FRACTURED COVENANTS

The Hidden Problem of Marital Abuse in the Church

FRACTURED COVENANTS

The Hidden Problem
of Marital Abuse
in the Church

MARIE O'TOOLE

© Calvary Press Publishing 2017

Calvarypress.com

1-855-2-CALVARY/855-222-5827

Published by Calvary Press

Copyright © Calvary Press Publishing

Interior design/cover: Raspberry Creative Type

ISBN 978-0-9973399-2-5

PRINTED IN THE USA

Dedication

This book is dedicated to the young mothers helped by Give Her Wings, and the tireless work of David and Megan Cox who have gone above and beyond the call of Christian duty to help them. These brave women, who have endured far worse situations than I, deserve compassion and recognition of their plight. I have tremendous respect for your ministry, which provides much-needed practical help to abused women – and gives a voice to the powerless.

Advance Praise for
Fractured Covenants:

"One of the greatest failures of the modern Church is its failure to understand, confront and respond to the horrors of domestic abuse – whether physical, verbal, or emotional. As a result, wounded women (and men) are so often left to suffer in silence while being pressured to remain or reconcile with the empowered abuser. Those who step forward are oftentimes ignored or even find themselves being the target of church discipline. This has been the tragic journey of Marie O'Toole and so many, many other women inside the Church. Marie has taken her experience and written this amazingly informative and helpful book that helps readers understand the evils associated with this offense, and the immense harm that is caused when we fail to respond to it in an informed and appropriate manner. I believe that *Fractured Covenants* has the potential to transform our churches into communities of refuge and unconditional support for victims of all forms of mistreatment, while ensuring that abusers are confronted, reported, and held accountable. Bravo Marie!"

Basyle 'Boz' Tchividjian,

Executive Director, G.R.A.C.E. (Godly Response to Abuse in the Christian Environment) and Professor of Law, Liberty University School of Law

"Trained as a nouthetic counselor, Marie O'Toole knows this counseling method well from the inside, which puts her in a position to be able to explain how harmful it can be in in cases of abuse—and she does that through telling her very own story. This description and analysis of her church's mishandling of her own personal situation at the hands of an abuser makes her book a truly worthwhile contribution to the ongoing conversation regarding the massive twin problems of domestic abuse in Christian homes and religious abuse at the hands of church leaders. This book will help readers understand and take action to bring truth and light into the churches and homes of Jesus Christ."

Rebecca Davis

Author of *Untwisting Scriptures*, co-author of *Unholy Charade: Unmasking the Domestic Abuser in the Church* and *Tear Down this Wall of Silence*

"Great work...may the Lord bless you and use the book for much good in exposing evil and setting the oppressed free!"

Jeff Crippin, Pastor of Christ Reformation Church (Tillamook, Oregon) and author of *A Cry for Justice: How the Evil of Domestic Abuse Hides in Your Church* and co-author of *Unholy Charade: Unmasking the Domestic Abuser in the Church*

Table of Contents

A Note from the Publisher

What do you do when the person who is supposed to love, lead and protect you in a God honoring way becomes the individual you fear the most? When your husband—or wife—becomes an abuser and will not listen to reason, who do you turn to? Well, if you are a committed Christian, you should turn immediately to your Lord and Savior in prayer. Your next thought would be to get help from your pastor and your local church. But... what if they not only don't help, but actually *protect* the abuser?

Many woman (and men) have experienced this disheartening and soul-crushing situation from the fellowship they surely thought would give them guidance and comfort.

Author Marie O'Toole is not simply writing about this problem from an intellectual, "Ivy tower" point of view, she has actually *lived* it! She spent many days trying to, at first, reason with her husband and reconcile. When this failed she turned to her church, who not only did not acknowledge her spouse's abusive behavior, but actually turned the tables and made *her out to be the one with the discipline problem*!

This book is not a tome against pastors, churches, marriage—or men. Rather, it is a clarion call to the Church to be aware of the calculating influence of abusers, and to not take Scripture, as it pertains to marriage and relationships, out of context. It is sounding the alarm bell to awaken the Church not only to the abuse that goes on between married couples in its midst, but often times to its own inaction when abused spouses come to them for help. Will they be believed, or will the situation be lightly brushed off as an "exaggeration"?

Joseph M. Bianchi, President
Calvary Press Publishing
November, 2017

Foreword

When Isaiah foretold the coming of the Christ, he put it in these glorious words:

> *The Spirit of the Lord God is upon me, Because the LORD has anointed me To bring good news to the afflicted; He has sent me to bind up the brokenhearted, To proclaim liberty to captives, And freedom to prisoners;*
>
> *² To proclaim the favorable year of the LORD, And the day of vengeance of our God; To comfort all who mourn,*
>
> *³ To grant those who mourn in Zion, Giving them a garland instead of ashes, The oil of gladness instead of mourning, The mantle of praise instead of a spirit of fainting. So they will be called oaks of righteousness, The planting of the LORD, that He may be glorified (Isaiah 61:1-3).*

What a tremendous blessing this would have been to the faithful remnant of the time. The poor were afflicted by the rich; the weak oppressed by the strong. The ignorant despised and the hopeless were mocked.

But the day would come when their Champion would arise "with healing in his wings" (Mal. 4:2). There is good news for the afflicted and liberty to the captives.

When Jesus first announced the kingdom of God in Galilee, he quoted this prophecy in Isaiah, and said: "Today this Scripture has been fulfilled in your hearing" (Luke 4:21).

To Jesus, the good news of the kingdom is nothing less than the deliverance of the captives and hope for the oppressed. The good news is joy to the mourners and gladness to the fainting.

Something has happened to the Church since then. Many are suffering from abuse of all kinds and the Church ignores their cries. The afflicted are excommunicated and the oppressors are praised.

Something is dreadfully wrong.

You won't find many in leadership who will say that abuse is acceptable. No, they generally condemn every kind of abuse with harsh language. But in practice, they do not live up to the Gospel that they proclaim. When large ministries are threatened in the eyes of the leadership, the poor and afflicted are hidden carefully away. When the wolves are carefully disguised, the vulnerable sheep are driven away and the shepherds grow fatter. And the huge wheels of the "ministry machine" continue to turn; conferences are packed with paying attendees; books are sold; reputations are made.

And the sheep are broken and battered outside the door. Just like the Levite and his father-in-law, the privileges ones rest in the house while the concubine is abused to death with her hands grasping the threshold of the door (see Judges 19-20).

But Jesus turns this on its head. It is the poor who are blessed; the meek (afflicted) who inherit the kingdom; the hungry who are filled; the mourners who end up learning to laugh.

What happened to the Church, who was to be the pillar and ground of God's people?

When the watchman cries out warning to the city of the wolves in the midst, there are generally two reactions. The first, from the wolves themselves in places of leadership. They revile, snarl, attack and lie to hold onto their positions of power. This book will do very little for them. They will respond as they are accustomed to responding: with rage and violence.

But there are also those who simply do not believe that this could happen in their circles. They speak loudly of abuse, but cannot – or *will* not – see it in their own pews.

"This couldn't happen here", they say in their hearts. "Maybe to others. Not here."

They usually think that the watchmen on the tower are exaggerating, blowing things out of proportion, crying wolf when there is no wolf.

But there are wolves. There are many wolves. Jesus warned us of them. Paul warned us. John warned us. So did Hosea, Jeremiah, Amos, Joel, Isaiah, Peter, Matthew, Luke, Mark…

I could continue, for the warning against the sons of Belial, the children of the devil, wolves in sheep's clothing – whichever term you use – is written in virtually every book of the Bible. It jumps off the pages, cries out for attention, begs a listener…if only we had eyes to see.

God told the serpent of old, "And I will put enmity between you and the woman." That enmity continues and will continue until the end, when we all finally crush his head under our feet together with our Lord Jesus Christ, the King of Kings, and Lord of Lords.

In *"Fractured Covenants"*, Marie is seeking to open your eyes to the wiles of the devil in our midst. Will you listen? When you read what she has thoroughly documented, you should be able to say, "No such thing ought to be done in Israel" (2 Sam. 13:12).

And yet it is done. The Church is under siege from within, and we refuse to hear. Now we need to learn to hear the cries of the oppressed – both by marital and spiritual abuse. We need to listen and watch. We need to examine the Scriptures and bring our thoughts captive to the Word of God. Are we faithfully proclaiming liberty to the captives and good news to the afflicted? If we are not, we are not proclaiming the Gospel of Jesus Christ.

If you are suffering, Marie portrays Christ as He is. He is your hope and your foundation. He will bring vengeance. He will bring healing in His wings.

He will never leave you or forsake you, for He has promised. And God cannot lie.

Reverend Sam Powell, First Reformed Church of Yuba City, CA
Blogs at: https://myonlycomfort.com

Introduction

When the president of Calvary Press contacted me to suggest I write a book about the forms of abuse Christian women experience, I was initially uncertain on how or whether to proceed. Shortly beforehand, my pastor and I had been discussing ways I might be able to help other women through my writing and speaking engagements, but at the time, the storm in my own life had not yet passed. I had myself been in a verbally and emotionally abusive marriage for two decades. Re-living traumatic experiences before one has fully healed can be triggering, and it is difficult to speak words of life and hope to others when one is running low on hope herself. However, marital abuse (of varying forms and degrees) has reached an epidemic level in this country, including within the Church. Countless women in conservative evangelical churches, where "male headship" is taught as a doctrine of primary importance, look to their husbands to see Christ's love. All too often, what they see instead is someone they have learned to fear. Staying silent is not an option.

A challenge inherent in writing about such a sensitive issue from one's own experience is to avoid sounding vindictive in any way. This book should not be read as a personal narrative, but rather as a well-researched treatment of an ugly problem with which I have some first-hand involvement. Where I have shared sufficient, but not exhaustive, detail about some of the sinful actions others chose to take against me, it is not with a motive to expose or embarrass. Rather, given the commonalities with other survivors' experiences, it is with a desire to educate, equip and empower women who are victimized and feel they have no choices. Secondly, it is my hope that clergy and others in Christian ministry will gain insight into what emotional abuse is, and how to truly help women rather than shaming or injuring them further.

Striving to Please…and Hoping for Change

Neither an autobiography nor a vendetta, the information in this book came as much from the shattered women I have counseled (or received messages from) as it did from my own experience. There is no one pattern or scenario that matches everyone's situation precisely, and it should not be assumed that women in destructive relationships are ready to give up and are simply looking for an excuse to leave. On the contrary, we all long for the type of loving, Christ-honoring marriages portrayed in ladies' Bible studies. We have embraced the calling to strive, pray, work and fast toward the goal of being "helpmeets" to our husbands; eager to "win [our husbands] over without a word"; to be the soothing influence needed to salve their anger and flaws. So many Christian women, married to angry men whose idols are power and control, are taught that if they just try *hard enough*, he will change.

Emotionally abused women want desperately to believe that their husbands love them. More than that, they want to believe that *God* loves them. During the explosive tirades or days-long silent treatments – which can be brought on for anything from under-cooking the potatoes to defending a child's error in judgement – a devout woman will almost believe that her husband speaks for God. If he, a mere mortal, could be that contemptuous towards his wife (who in theory he was supposed to love,) how much less must God think of her?

Much of the teaching and books aimed at evangelical women prime us to accept (and enable) abusive husbands. When the majority of Christian marriage books emphasize meek submission to the exclusion of men being called to account for their anger, adultery, or other sins against their wives, the wives are being conditioned to accept any mistreatment they receive as God's will. Far from being a balanced, biblical picture of complementarianism, patriarchal authoritarian teaching sets the stage for marital abuse. And when it occurs, it will be shrouded in secrecy and most likely swept under the rug.

The Way Out

Over the years I grew in my identity in Christ and was able to discern the power of God's love. I never doubted His care and protection of the vulnerable (including wives with smashed spirits). Yet countless Christian women remain trapped in this bondage. Some are beaten; deprived economically (withholding household budget money from women with no income of their own is a common abuse tactic); some are relentlessly tormented with intimidation, constant criticism, humiliation (especially in front of their children), rages, and false accusations. And then they are bullied into believing the abusive tirade was somehow all their fault. "Well, I wouldn't *have* to get so angry, if you didn't *make* me!" There is an enormous difference between a disappointing marriage, and a destructive one. Women in abusive marriages are in the latter category.

As an evangelical woman with a vibrant ministry and membership in a conservative church, I knew it wouldn't be easy to end this destructive relationship and heal spiritually. Yet I knew that God was with me, and as a scrupulously honest and transparent person, I believed that if I divulged sufficient detail with my then-church leaders, they would support and help me through this difficult time. Unfortunately, this was not the case. While I was blessed to have the support of strong Christian friends and counselors, my family, and the new church community which embraced me, it is all too common for women asking for help to be dismissed or disbelieved (especially if the abuse is not physical). Many women fleeing to protect themselves and their children face abject poverty. Although secular organizations, shelters, and independent Christian ministries (such as Give Her Wings) come to the aid of abused women, sadly, their local churches often turn a blind eye to their plight. Worse, the counsel to marital abuse victims in many churches is dangerously unbiblical and destructive.

When Abuse is Tolerated, it Flourishes

It seems counter-intuitive that the Christian Church, long regarded as a place of healing, refuge and protection of the weak would be a place where abuse (of different forms) is not only tolerated, but very much enabled by some of her leaders. They thus add secondary *spiritual* abuse onto the terrible wounds already caused by the destructive marriage. Moreover, it is usually the one exposing the unbiblical (and sometimes even unlawful) actions who is castigated by the local church. Often, exposing spiritual abuse is seen as a greater evil than the abusive behavior itself.

In *The Voices of Redlands*, a memoir of his excommunication for exposing the heresy of Hyper-Grace taught in his California house church, Ryan Ashton writes:

> I confess I have been profoundly baffled by the lukewarm love of Christians who recognize the problems [of spiritual abuse] but do nothing to stop it; who are more devoted to the shackles of conformity under the guise of "unity" than to the dignifying freedom of truth; who believe the existing conditions are acceptable despite the absence of resolution; who prefer we remain silent rather than speak; who are more cautious than courageous; who say "I agree with the goal you seek, but not

the way you are going about it"; and who believe more harm is created by exposing evil than allowing it to fester.[1]

The bystander effect happens every time a church-goer or neighbor notices a woman's bruises, fearful countenance, or skittishness around her husband... and says nothing. It happens when she confides the toxic nature of her marriage to her Bible study leader, and is told to "pray more" or "be more available" to her husband. It happens when sexual assaults are not reported (and victims are told to "turn the other cheek"), because going to the local authorities is seen in some circles as a greater sin than the actual sin of assault. Averting our eyes when one of our sisters is being abused, in any form, is not Christ-like.

While the main focus of this book is on the non-physical ways women are often mistreated in Christian marriages, physical and sexual abuse are harsh realities within the Church as well. If you or someone you know is being abused in this way, go straight to the police and file a report. Do *not* wait for your abuser to repent, change, or minimize his behavior – you need to protect yourself *now*.

Victim-Blaming and Spiritual Abuse

One of the ways the Church has greatly failed its most vulnerable members is in failing to confront abuse sufficiently or biblically. As pastor Jeff Crippin has written about at length in his books *A Cry for Justice* and *Unholy Charade*, one of the unflattering aspects of conservative Christianity in the United States (particularly in churches in the Reformed/Neo-Calvinist camp) is its tendency to pursue the *victim* of abuse (usually a woman) for "church discipline". After having endured years and sometimes decades of abuse in her marriage, a woman separating or filing for divorce may often expect further torment from the very church leaders she trusted to protect and defend her. She essentially faces two choices: return to her abuser; or be excommunicated. The woman usually has to leave the church, while the relentless contact urging "reconciliation" is termed 'pursuing her in love'. Finally, she is shunned – a pariah among the believers she once trusted as brothers and sisters.

The word picture *"broken toys"* is an apt analogy for those of us who, already hurting over the mistreatment in our marriages, bore the additional contempt of a church determined to cast us as the villains (while exonerating and embracing our abusers). The cognitive dissonance and feeling of betrayal

---

[1] Ryan Ashton, *The Voices of Redlands* (2016). Retrieved from http://redlandsbook. com

that spiritual abuse inflicts is especially toxic. Unlike physical abuse, which can easily be identified as reprehensible and without justification, spiritual abuse is insidious. It can make a victim question her salvation; relationship to God; even her own sanity. It is typical "gaslighting" (crazy-making) activity. Many of us bear the scars inflicted by misguided spiritual leaders who, rather than caring for and supporting us, castigated and shamed us for standing up and speaking out.

Fortunately, the widespread problem of domestic abuse within Christian marriages is beginning to get the attention it deserves. In addition to Crippin, ministry leaders such as Sam Powell, Leslie Vernick, Ashley Easter, and a growing number of Protestant pastors in the United States and Australia are now speaking out about a problem once denied and kept under wraps. With increased media and ecclesiastical attention being focused on the issue, Christian ministry leaders may better learn what real abuse actually is, and re-think their doctrinal positions on how to advocate for the true victims.

It is my hope that all in ministry – pastors, small group leaders, and counselors alike – will read this book and consider how to help the many victims of marital abuse in their pews. Recognizing the signs of emotional abuse and considering how to confront it as the sin it is should be a mandatory component of true biblical counseling. How does Christ minister love, healing and grace to the abused and/or divorced woman? How should we?

CHAPTER 1

The Silent 50%

"The women are to keep silent in the churches;
for they are not permitted to speak, but are to subject
themselves, just as the Law also says."
(1 Corinthians 14:34)

For two millennia, the words of the apostle Paul to the unruly church of Corinth have been preached, exegeted, parsed, debated about, used as a conversation stopper, and pulled out as ammunition to keep "uppity women" in their place. The arguments for and against the meaning of this verse (and others from the New Testament pertaining to male authority) have been many. Some believe this was a culturally-relevant instruction to a First Century world that saw women as inferior; others point to the chaotic and subversive nature of certain women in the Corinthian church (and therefore see the instruction as specific to that congregation); others point to the Creation order as a foreshadowing of male headship in the Church, and take the verse literally for all times and all places.

Of course, all Scripture is God-breathed and is there for a reason. We cannot snip out portions of our Bible that we do not like (as Thomas Jefferson allegedly did); but rather, must read the whole of Scripture and see how other verses "line up" in the same way. The synthetic principle of hermeneutics ("Scripture interprets Scripture") is our friend. Or, as a pastor I know used to say, "Be careful of basing a doctrine on one verse."

Fortunately, we have far more than just one verse. When we study gender roles and Church leadership in the New Testament, I believe we are going to find several things.

- 1 Corinthians 14:34 does not exist in a vacuum.
- The New Testament Church was revolutionary in that it treated women as equals – being on equal footing in the Kingdom of

God (Galatians 3:28); recognizing their gifts (Acts 21:9; 9:36); and praising them for their character and ability to instill faith in their children (1 Peter 3:4; 2 Timothy 1:5).

- Jesus loved and ministered to women openly, in a gender-segregated society.
- Women like Priscilla (whose education and standing seems to have been above that of her husband's) were used to spread the Gospel in the Early Church, right alongside men (Acts 18:2-3, 26; Rom 16:3).
- God's design for overseers of the local church is for male pastors/elders (1 Corinthians 11:3; Ephesians 5:22; 1 Timothy 2:12).

When we look at Scripture, we see harmony. We see a God Who loves all His children equally; Who protects the weak; provides for the powerless; gives different strengths and abilities; gives unique talents. Who does not subscribe to man's political agendas or changing social standards. A loving Father Who despises abuse (Psalm 11:5; Malachi 2:16) and protects the innocent (Psalm 43:1, 82:3). Who does not condone using power to control/unjustly oppress others (Zechariah 7:10; Proverbs 22:22-23; Matthew 23:13-14:23).

True Biblical Submission

Christian counselor and writer Valerie Jacobsen describes true Christ-like submission this way: "Biblical submission is an aspect of Christian liberty wherein we prefer others to ourselves. It's an expression of Christian love, intended to glorify God in all that it chooses to do. It kindly and generously serves others, to provide for their comfort. It defers to others, it edifies them, and it blesses them according to their needs. It's genuinely benevolent and seeks the welfare and best interests of others. It diligently pursues life, health, and dignity for others as well as oneself. Biblical submission, far from being a sanctified form of dictatorship, honors God as supreme and honors others as his creatures made in his image."

Problems in interpretation do not lie with the verses themselves, or God's intent behind them. He need explain Himself to no one. The problem is with over-laying the Word of God with one's own agenda (eisegesis). As anyone familiar with biblical theology (and the verses most likely to spark debates) knows, almost any verse dealing with authority can be used as a weapon in the hands of someone whose end-goal is *control*.

Women comprise half the world's population. The intent of 1 Corinthians 14:34, taken within the historical context and placement in the text, clearly is to promote orderly learning and worship under the guidance of the more educated in the local church. Women were not in a position of teaching, and Paul was trying to prevent disruption of services while including both genders in the worship and study going on. Women were never excluded from worship, prevented from using their spiritual gifts, forbidden from proclaiming the Gospel or even teaching converts, as we have seen in the verses above. They were given equal footing in Christ, and were entrusted to the faithful, loving care of their (monogamous) husbands – a mind-boggling elevation of female status in the male-dominated Roman Empire.

Literally taking away our voice, or subjugating all women to second-class status in the Church was never Paul's intention by instituting male-lead church offices. On the contrary, the call to "silence" women – not just in co-ed Sunday school classes, but in the Body of Christ – has led to misogynistic attitudes that are anything but Christ-like. It is within this environment, still alive and well in branches of Christendom, where various types of abuse can flourish behind a mask of piety.

The Hi-Jacking of Ephesians 5:22

Before we look more closely at various forms of spousal abuse, let's examine one of the most-frequently cited passages of Scripture used to justify tyrannical and abusive behavior of men towards their wives. A young woman in a Bible study read the following passage from the book of Ephesians:

"Wives, submit to your own husbands, as to the Lord. For the husband is the head of the wife even as Christ is the head of the church, his body, and is himself its Savior. Now as the church submits to Christ, so also wives should submit in everything to their husbands." (Ephesians 5:22-24).

"I don't like that," she said. "It makes me uncomfortable."

Young lady, none of us likes it when words are given new connotations that God never intended; when verses are wrenched out of context and used to justify selfish desires. And it *should* make us uncomfortable when well-meaning Christians use "proof texts" to subjugate those weaker than themselves, or dismiss another human made in the image of God as inferior. This was never how marriage was designed. We need to see the beauty of the whole passage; what it means to submit to one another out of love and respect; and what God actually intended when He established the pattern of loving male leadership in the family (and in the Church).

The book of Ephesians is an outline of demonstrating *Christ-like love* in different relationships. Paul opens by exhorting the believers to avoid all forms of sexual immorality and indecent behavior, then zooms in on the nuclear family. After entrusting women to the authority of their husbands in the above passage, the Apostle then turns to the husbands and spends *three times* as much space commanding them to *"love their wives as Christ loved the Church"*. Neither a battle cry for feminism nor a return to draconian male-dominance, the entire passage simply reinforces Paul's original plea for *all* to "walk in love".

We women were created to serve next to (not behind) our men.

A Proof-Text for 'Control Issues'?

In the 1991 thriller *Sleeping with the Enemy*, Julia Roberts plays a wife who flees a man so controlling that he lectured her for bathroom towels being hung unevenly, and berated her for spices not lined up symmetrically in the pantry. The woman was so brow-beaten by his excessive control that she lived in constant fear and humiliation. This is an exaggerated picture of how non-Christians view biblical submission. Unfortunately, even among believers, the sin nature has sometimes distorted God's intention for submission and authority.

What often seems to be the case is that this passage is pulled out of context to force women into an unbiblical form of subjugation rooted *not* in sacrificial love, but rather in an egocentric desire for control. Verse 22 is often quoted as a conversation-stopper when wills collide, but verse 25 is often ignored. However inconvenient and embarrassing it may be, *spiritual abuse is real* – and is often rooted in an unbiblical application of Ephesians 5:22-24.

This is not to say, of course, that church-going men who autocratically rule their families are not "real Christians". On the contrary. In an *autocratic leadership,* the person in charge has total authority and control over decision making. There are many committed Christian men *who actually believe* this is God's will and model for family life, and are convinced it is their sacred responsibility to uphold the entire burden of doing, working, deciding – and even thinking. I have even seen an inflated sense of 'patriarchy' convince Christian husbands that their wives do not even have the right to *think* or make *any decisions* for the family, citing the principle of "submission" to rationalize their absolute power.

The Cycle of Abuse and Shame

This is not only poor exegesis, it is emotional abuse. A familial dictatorship is psychologically destructive, and is much more spiritually damaging to the woman than physical abuse. Here's why:

- Woman is being treated as second-class citizen at home; even if she holds academic degrees, may be subtly treated as of lower-intelligence;
- Woman reads literature targeted towards evangelical women, over-emphasizing "submission" in order to be a more 'godly wife';
- Woman begins to believe abuse is her fault, feels guilty;
- Woman gradually distances herself from God; feels she *deserves* the abuse and strives to be "better".

The problem with teaching absolute female submission is that when we lose sight of the heart-attitude Paul wants to instill – namely, *sacrificial, agape love for one another* – the true meaning of marriage is distorted. Everywhere in Scripture, we see Christ far more preoccupied with what's going on inside the soul than with outward behavior, and marital interaction is no exception. Marriage is supposed to mirror the relationship of Christ and His Bride, the Church. When the sin nature twists surrender to another's loving authority into a doormat theology, women suffer in silence; bitterness is fostered; abuse is legitimized; and those who slander Christianity gain more ammunition. (Last year's Vision Forum sexual abuse scandal was a prime example of this dynamic.)

Cycle of Abuse

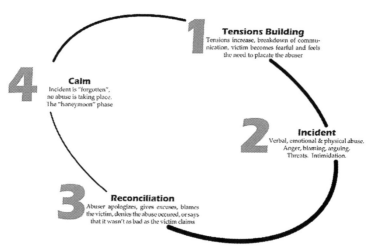

1 Tensions Building
Tensions increase, breakdown of communication, victim becomes fearful and feels the need to placate the abuser

4 Calm
Incident is "forgotten", no abuse is taking place. The "honeymoon" phase

2 Incident
Verbal, emotional & physical abuse. Anger, blaming, arguing. Threats. Intimidation.

3 Reconciliation
Abuser apologizes, gives excuses, blames the victim, denies the abuse occured, or says that it wasn't as bad as the victim claims

"Did Your Husband Speak for You?"

Several years ago, my then-husband and I had a doctrinal question for the leadership of our church. In the course of events, I was dialoguing about it with another woman, who was part of the "Family Integrated Church (FIC) movement. The FIC puts a very strong emphasis on male headship and has a narrow interpretation of "biblical womanhood" (a thorny issue we will examine in a later chapter). My former husband, who is less theologically-interested than I, had delegated the discussion to me. English is not his first language, and he knew I had good rapport with the counseling pastor. My friend was somewhat surprised that I, as a woman, would be "allowed to speak on my family's behalf" to church leadership.

I was at first amused, then incredulous. As an adult in my forties, a certified biblical counselor with a college degree, having raised four children and written two books while holding a full-time career, I need *permission from my husband* to have a conversation with our pastor? Whether or not he had delegated the issue to me, have branches of American evangelicalism reverted so far back into medieval authoritarianism that a woman discussing theology with her pastor raises eyebrows? Where, exactly, is the biblical precedent for this?

If we return to the pages of the New Testament, we see that Jesus Himself held no such views of women having an inferior status, intellectually or socially. Several women travelled with Jesus and His disciples during His ministry, listened to His teaching and "provided for them *out of their means.*" (Luke 8:3, emphasis mine.) We see the disciples surprised that Jesus would converse with a woman (John 4:27) and the dignity He afforded women went far beyond the conventions of 1st Century Judea (John 8:11; Luke 7:48; Mark 14:6; etc.) And this does not even scratch the surface of the role women played in the Early Church.

The Pendulum Swing

Where, then, does the desire to return to an absolute patriarchy (with women forbidden a say in the family, or critical thinking, even if they have higher education) come from? It is possible that it is a knee-jerk reaction to the extremes of the feminist movement, which would deny the God-given differences (in nature and role) between men and women. This is a sociological explanation, and I believe it has some validity given that liberalism has invaded the Church in the last three decades. However, it falls short of a biblical solution and does not help us address the problem of spiritual abuse in the counseling room or the family. Current patriarchy is a cultural bastardization of Augustine's neo-platoism which believed women were sub-human, deformed males. In an over-correction of the extremes of feminism, the conservative evangelical world has birthed a theology that teaches women are to be not only silent, but servile as well.

Love is not self-seeking, and it does not "lord it over" another individual – especially one perceived as weaker. Love protects, and it seeks the other's best interest. While women are called to submit, it should never be done in slavish fear to an autocrat – but rather in joyful deference to the one she trusts above all else; who would lay down his life for her. When a command for submission is wielded like a weapon, it is a sure sign that the follow-up verses on "loving [your] wife as Christ loved the Church" are not being obeyed. Christ never intimidates or threatens the Church. Rather, He encourages believers to use their gifts in His service; always heals; always protects.

While there are many causes of emotional abuse within Christian marriages, I believe that the misunderstanding and misuse of this particular passage of Scripture is behind much of it. Women should not be conditioned either from the pulpit or by strong-willed men to think of themselves as "lesser"; but rather should be edified and uplifted by their true identity in Christ. One of the ways to break this stranglehold is to encourage a woman to develop and use her individual gifts and talents, *not only within the family setting,* but in the Church and culture as a whole.

What is Abuse?

I deliberately wanted to set the stage for any discussion of marital abuse by laying out the biblical pattern of marriage and how it can be twisted. Once we can see marriage as God intended it, without lenses distorting the husband-wife relationship into a 'servant-master' dynamic, we can more easily identify the subtler forms of emotional abuse.

Physical abuse, which is much more overt, does of course exist within Christian marriages. It would include any use of force or bodily intimidation, from open-handed slaps to beatings; obstructing another (in order to intimidate); or any of the myriad ways we can imagine a person to do violence to another. Wife-beating is not something unique to unbelievers. While the Bible may never prescribe beating one's wife as the Koran does (Surah 4:34), unfortunately there are many Christian men who misguidedly believe that keeping a woman "in submission" includes slapping, spanking, hitting, beating, and other criminal activities.

However, much more common in Western Christian families is a power dynamic we would call "emotional abuse". The probate court system calls this "mental abuse"; the mental health profession cites "psychological abuse"; and at least one well-known nouthetic[2] counseling leader calls it mythical ("There is no such thing as emotional abuse, because emotions cannot be abused"). When I was training to become a nouthetic counselor, this statement (and many others like it) struck me as overly-simplistic and concerning. A high school classmate who escaped an emotionally-abusive marriage to a very controlling man wrote me, "Men who verbally abuse are insidious and don't back down too easily. They want to "win" at all costs, and will continue to find ways to beat you down into submission. Verbal/emotional abuse is incredibly hard and not to equate it to the pain of physical abuse, but it's so much harder to explain to people...for people to take it seriously."

What Does the Bible Say about Abuse?

Abuse literally means to mistreat someone, although we often think of 'abuse' as being merely physical. Mistreatment or abuse of other people is sinful for two reasons: firstly, because humans are created in the image of God; and secondly, because abuse is always motivated by *selfishness* and results in damage and destruction. People abuse others for a variety of reasons, but selfishness underlies all mistreatment. When we mishandle anger, it leads to an abusive, sinful response. The heart issue is rooted in pride: putting one's self above another; disregarding his or her feelings; and ignoring the command of God to love one another (John 13:34; Luke 6:31). The Bible strongly condemns abusing or cheating others (Exodus 22:22; Isaiah 10:2; 1 Thessalonians 4:6), and in fact, 1 John 4:20 calls a person who claims to love God but abuses (hates) another a "liar."

Men who verbally abuse their wives are what the Bible calls "revilers". A reviler is one who is deliberately abusive in their speech. Pastor Sam Powell of Yuba City's First Reformed Church writes:

> A reviler is one who uses speech to vomit out their anger, to tear down and destroy, and to belittle and condemn. A reviler doesn't leave physical bruises, but seeks to silence and degrade the image of God in their target. The church at Corinth was being rebuked by the Apostle for being too proud to remove the corrupt leaven.

---

2 Nouthetic counseling (from Greek: *noutheteo*, to admonish) is a form of evangelical Protestant pastoral counseling based solely upon the Bible. It repudiates mainstream psychology and psychiatry as humanistic, fundamentally opposed to Christianity, and radically secular. There are other forms of Christian counseling which rely on the Bible, but also incorporate insights from clinical psychology and take a more integrated approach to the individual.

He doesn't use fists, for he is skilled at destructive speech. He comes to church every Sunday and professes Christ. According to this text, he is a reviler, who calls himself a brother. So, what does this passage say? "Don't even eat with this guy. He will corrupt the whole church."[3]

Examples of emotional abuse include verbal attacks, silent treatment, destructive criticism, manipulation, lying, threats, and withholding affection. These toxic relationships affect the victim's ability to trust others and enjoy healthy relationships in the future. Domestic violence isn't just about punching/hitting. *It's about power and control.*

Universally considered to be the preeminent expert in the field of abuse, Lundy Bancroft provides a much more specific and comprehensive breakdown of the forms emotional abuse takes in his book *Why Does He Do That? Inside the Minds of Angry and Controlling Men*:

Where Does Subtler Mistreatment End, and Abuse Begin?

- He retaliates against you for complaining about his behavior. Suppose you complain about being silenced by his constant interruptions. He then gets a huffy, hostile tone in his voice as if your objection were unfair to him and says sarcastically, "All right, I'll just listen and you talk," and acts as if you are oppressing him by calling him on his behavior.

- He tells you that your objections to his mistreatment are your problem. He says such things as: "You're too sensitive; every little thing bothers you." "Not everyone is all nicey-nice when they're angry like you want them to be," or "You're just getting angry because you're not getting your way, so you're saying I'm mistreating you."

- Through comments like these, the abuser can try to persuade you that: 1) you have unrealistic expectations for his behavior, and you should be willing to live with the things that he does; 2) you are actually reacting to something else in your life, not to what he did; and 3) you are using your grievances as a power move against him. All of these tactics are forms of discrediting your complaints of mistreatment, which is abusive. His discrediting maneuvers reveal a core attitude: "…you have no right to object to how I treat you." And you can't be in a fair and healthy relationship if you can't raise grievances.

3   https://myonlycomfort.com/2017/06/02/christians-who-revile/

- He gives apologies that sound insincere or angry, and he demands that you accept them. The abuser may add angry insults and crazy-making denial about whatever she was already upset about. He feels she should be grateful for his apology, even though his tone communicated the opposite of his words; he in fact feels entitled to forgiveness, and he demands it.

- He blames you for the impact of his behavior. He becomes upset and accusatory when his partner exhibits the predictable effects of chronic mistreatment, and then he adds insult to injury by ridiculing her for feeling hurt by him. If his verbal assaults cause her to lose interest in sex with him, he says, "You must be getting it somewhere else."

- It's never the right time, or the right way, to bring things up. With an abuser, no way to bring up a complaint is the right way. You can wait until the calmest, most relaxed evening, prepare your partner with plenty of verbal stroking, express your grievance in mild language, but he still won't be willing to take it in.

- He undermines your progress in life. He takes advantage of you financially, interferes with your job or your school, causes damage to your relationships, and tells you that you are incompetent at something you enjoy.

- He denies what he did. A non-abusive partner might argue with you about how you interpret something he did; an abuser denies his actions altogether.

- He justifies his hurtful actions or says you "made him do it." Here the abuser is using your behavior as an excuse for his own....He says he'll stop some form of abuse if you give up something that bothers him, which is usually something you have every right to do.

- He touches you in anger or makes you fearful in other ways. Physical aggression by a man toward a woman is abuse, even if it happens only once. He raises a fist; he punches a wall, throws things at you; blocks your way; restrains you; grabs, pushes, or pokes you; threatens to hurt you. That is physical abuse. No assault in a relationship, however "minor," should be taken lightly.

- His controlling, disrespectful, or degrading behavior is a pattern. [4]

---

[4] Lundy Bancroft, *Why Does He Do That? Inside the Minds of Angry and Controlling Men* (New York: G.P. Putman's Sons, 2002), 125-128.

The question then arises, "Why would a Christian woman, well-versed in Scripture, tolerate this kind of behavior?" This is a complex question, which we will examine more closely in a later chapter when we look at how conservative Christian women are conditioned by the teaching of (often godly) teachers to accept and even enable their abusive husbands' behavior. For now, we need to shine light on the problem: first, by acknowledging that spousal abuse does exist within the Church; secondly, by examining specific manifestations of such torment; and thirdly, by recognizing that even some respected Christian teachers do not consider domestic abuse that big of a deal.

Endure for a Season?

Why some men choose to exert their control over women and hurt them (either physically or emotionally) is a complicated question we will unpack in this book. What is alarming, however, is the response of many respected Christian leaders to the problem of domestic abuse that runs rampant through the pews of their churches. John Piper, for example, was asked in a recorded 2009 interview "What should a wife's submission to her husband look like if he's an abuser?" Piper's first concern was not for the woman's well-being, but whether she were being "asked to engage in abusive or weird acts, such as group sex", which would, of course, be dishonoring to Christ. Her response to her husband should be sweet, deferential, and almost apologetic when she declines. He then stated, "If it's not requiring her to sin, but simply *hurting her*, then I think she endures verbal abuse for a season, she endures perhaps being *smacked* one night, and then she seeks help from the church."[5]

This was an extremely naïve and telling statement. Piper clearly does not understand the ongoing nature or emotional toll that physical abuse takes, and shows appalling disregard for the reality abused women endure. "*Simply* hurting her?" The many forms of abuse a man can inflict on his wife are despised by God, who has commanded husbands to protect, honor and love their wives (Colossians 3:19; Ephesians 5:25, 28; Proverbs 5:18-19; Ephesians 5:33). He refuses even to hear the prayer of a man who mistreats his wife (1 Peter 3:7). Nowhere in Scripture is a women charged to "endure for a season" while the man God has given her to love torments her. (In 2012, Piper did qualify his statements somewhat in another sermon, conceding that physical abuse is a misdemeanor and a woman has the right to go to the civil authorities. Slight progress, perhaps?)[6]

[5]   https://www.youtube.com/watch?v=3OkUPc2NLrM

[6]   http://www.desiringgod.org/articles/clarifying-words-on-wife-abuse

16

While Piper's appeal to the local church for aid sounds reasonable on the surface, the sad reality is that many conservative churches are woefully ill-equipped to provide help (either spiritual or practical) to women who have been abused. Even when I was taking courses to become a nouthetic counselor, I was struck by how spousal abuse (particularly of the non-physical kind) was glossed over in lectures. The advice offered to women in such situations boiled down to "go to the local church for help; read 1 Peter on 'suffering for the sake of righteousness'; pray more." In the 185 lecture hours I took, domestic abuse was only mentioned once, and the existence of emotional abuse was denied ("Emotions cannot be abused").

It was implied that the wife should remain silent unless the abuse were endangering her physically, "so that she may win [her husband] over without a word". Again, this misuse of 1 Peter 3:1 emphasized silencing the woman. Keep quiet about what's going on; try harder; don't speak up. In chapter 3, we will examine some of the common statements made to women that condition them to accept abuse and to feel it is their own fault, but for now we may see that keeping a code of silence allows mistreatment to grow unchecked.

Of course, there are many good courses of study for Christian counseling offered through different organizations. Nowadays more attention is being given to the problem of emotional abuse by organizations such as the American Association of Christian Counselors (AACC) and the Christian Counseling & Educational Foundation (CCEF). However, there is still a huge disconnect between society at large (which acknowledges that women in destructive marriages need help), and the response of the Church – which, all too often, minimizes the abuse; blames the victim; or attempts to force reconciliation with the perpetrator before any real change has occurred. In the next chapter, we will look more closely at the forms emotional and psychological abuse takes, and their prevalence within authoritarian Christian marriages.

CHAPTER 2
Types of Emotional Abuse

"Love cherishes and finds pleasure in the pleasure of another. It serves and delights to honor. Hatred (abuse), however, loves to say no and withhold. It loves to say, "Only I matter." It loves to injure, curse, and starve. It loves to cause pain and finds pleasure in the suffering of another. With twisted avarice, it craves service and loves to humiliate. This is the nature and character of good and evil, and it's why the Bible doesn't present a comprehensive system that will work for every marriage or relationship."
– Testimony of an abuse survivor

"Brenda" was married for 22 years to a man who constantly criticized her. "Are you sure you should be eating that? You are too fat!" He would over-control every aspect of her day, to the point she felt like his slave. Finally, one night in a drunken stupor, he told her "Get out! I cannot live with such a fat, ugly wife anymore."

"Donna" never remembers her parents hugging her, or telling her that they loved her growing up. Her father and brother started calling her a cruel nickname to taunt her: "hopeless, helpless and useless." For years, she walked with her head down – ashamed to make eye contact with anyone.

"Anna" was in love with a young man – who was in love with himself. Angry outbursts; threats to "leave" and erratic, self-centered behavior came to be the norm for Anna. "He's just a 'complicated' person," she would rationalize. "I know that he loves me!"

Although they were never hit or beaten, these three women shared something in common: they were emotionally abused. All types of emotional abuse are rooted in *pride* and *selfish desires* (James 4:1), and create shame in their victims. Christians who have been hurt (whether by parents, dating relationships, or in marriage) feel the sting of harsh words and betrayal just as strongly as anyone. This kind of pain lasts much longer than the bruises of being hit, and can only be forgiven and healed with the help and hope of Christ.

Within the Family

The most common form of emotional abuse is verbal – and the effects of hurtful words linger for years. Parents sometimes underestimate the destructive power of words spoken in anger, or the ability of children to remember destructive criticism for decades. The Bible warns fathers (and by implication, mothers) against embittering their children by the way they treat them (Ephesians 6:4, Colossians 3:21). Being repeatedly shamed by their parents or being held to an impossibly-high standard often causes children to view God as a distant or cruel task-master. Christian counselor David Powlinson quotes a woman he counseled in *Life Beyond Your Parents' Mistakes*:

> For years I thought I could never know God as my Father because I had such a rotten relationship with my dad. But then I came to realize that my biggest problem was me, not God or my father. My belief system was all messed up. I was projecting lies onto God and not believing what was true about him!' Sally began to feed her faith with the truth that God the Father is faithful, merciful, and consistent. He patiently worked with her, disciplining her and teaching her to know the merciful, generous truth about him. Sally saw that her view of God was not caused by her life experience but by what her own heart had done with her experience of being wronged.[7]

The Silent Marriage-Killer

God's plan for a happy married life that honors Him is best laid out in Ephesians 5, which we have already considered. Husbands are instructed to love their wives sacrificially – and wives are to submit to their husbands out of respect for their spiritual authority. Sadly, many spouses – even Christian ones – are living in a reality far different. When a woman is beaten, her plight is less likely to go unnoticed and the local church (as well as police) may become involved. Emotional abuse, while just as painful, is much harder to detect. Even her closest friends may not know, because the victim

---

[7]   David Powlinson, *Life Beyond Your Parents' Mistakes* (Greensboro: New Growth Press, 2010), 23.

is conditioned into believing it is deserved or is somehow her[8] fault. Shame is a crippling effect of abuse of all types.

What makes verbal abuse so damaging is that it is *intentional*. The power of one's words over another must not be minimized. The Bible tells us "the power of life and death is in the tongue" (Proverbs 18:21) and that the tongue, while small, can "set a forest on fire" (James 3:5). Instead of encouraging and building up, abusive spouses humiliate and tear down with their words. Constant and personal criticism; power plays; and intimidation destroys trust and intimacy. One pastor and counselor had this to say about verbal abuse within families, and marriage in particular:

> The matter [of verbal abuse] is not really mentioned in the Old Testament, but it is in the New. In fact, we have the opportunity to compare many types of relationships. In Ephesians 5:22 – 6:9, for example, Paul rules out abusive speech in three types of relationships.
>
> (1) The husband (5:25 – 33) is not to accuse his wife, thereby separating himself emotionally from her in violation of the head-body unity of marriage. He is to speak to her with the same intent that Jesus had for His Church: to wash the Church with His Word. That is, Jesus speaks to the Church not to condemn her, but to express His unity with her in love and build her up.
>
> (2) The father (6:4) is not to exasperate, anger, or embitter his children but to teach them patiently.
>
> (3) The master (6:9) is to 'do the same' as the slave in what the slave was commanded (!), i.e. respect, fear, serve with sincerity, and additionally, 'to give up threatening.'
>
> In each of these three cases, physical, cultural, and/or legal power is subverted for a distinctly Christian purpose, especially regarding how we speak. This is what leads the Christian community into being a community where songs of praise and a symphony of thanksgiving break forth from everyone, the vision of the Church that Paul gives in Eph.5:18 – 20 right before talking about these three relationships where power is involved. The Church is to be a singing symphony where we all have a part. To be 'filled by the Spirit' as Paul says (5:18)

---

[8]   Because most victims of marital abuse are women, I generally use female pronouns in this book to refer to them and male pronouns to refer to the abuser. However, some verbally and emotionally abused spouses are men, a topic we will consider in chapter 5.

is to be a community where *all* speak, not just the powerful. Regardless of what exactly one's views of "headship" means for a husband's relationship to his wife, one thing should be quite obvious: verbal abuse is clearly sinful.[9]

There are several types of emotional abusers in marriage and romantic relationships. Let's look briefly at three.

The Tyrant

Tyrants hold power over their subjects by fear and intimidation. The most common form of emotional abuse they use is verbal – a constant stream of insults, put-down, threats and even false accusations to achieve their ends. A tyrant is usually a very angry person, believing he deserves more than what God has sovereignly provided. A woman married to a tyrannical husband often lives in fear, as his temper may be volatile and unpredictable.

Towards the end of my marriage, I was told that I did not have the right to authority in the household because I earned less money than my then-husband. He had previously forbidden me to make any decisions that affected the family (every single thing was to come through him first), and I was to "leave all the thinking to him." It was not like this in the early days of our marriage, but controlling men usually grow in tyranny the more power the wife relinquishes to them. Her days are clouded in fear.

The Manipulator

> Manipulators suck time and energy out of your life under the façade of friendship. They can be tricky to deal with because they treat you like a friend, but have a hidden agenda. Manipulators always want something from you, and if you look back on your relationships with them, it's all take, take, take with little or no giving. They'll do anything to win you over just so they can work you over. (Dr. Travis Bradberry, Ph.d) [10]

Manipulation is often more obvious to people outside the relationship than it is to the person being abused in this way. The person being manipulated wants desperately to believe she is loved, but the manipulator uses others only so long as he can gain something from the relationship.

---

[9] Mako Nagasaw, personal correspondence with author.

[10] http://www.talentsmart.com/articles/10-Toxic-People-You-Should-Avoid-At-All-Costs

The Narcissist

The narcissist is incapable of loving anyone but himself. He has a delusional, inflated view of his own achievements and character; a legend in his own mind who deserves the adulation of others. In 2 Timothy 3, Paul warns Timothy of those within the Church who act out of an attitude of "self-love". He describes narcissists as "lovers of themselves, lovers of money, boasters, proud, blasphemers, disobedient to parents, unthankful, unholy, unloving, unforgiving, slanderers, without self-control, brutal, despisers of good, traitors, headstrong, haughty, lovers of pleasure rather than lovers of God."

Narcissists do not form healthy relationships, because they are utterly self-absorbed and lack empathy (or interest) in other people. Other traits of a narcissist include preoccupation with unlimited success, belief that he is special and unique, exploitation of others, a lack of empathy, arrogance, and jealousy of others.

Narcissistic Personality Disorder, or NPD, has been classified by the DSM-5 as a mental condition, and most abusers are broadly assumed to be narcissists. However, a clinical diagnosis seems out of place for one with these characteristics – he is simply deep in sin with a delusional view of his own importance. This is why he tries so hard to control other people. As a worshipper of himself, the narcissist must have others serve and bow down to him at all costs. Power is his drug.

Christ's Response to Abusers

When we turn to the Bible, we see that Christ Himself was no stranger to verbal abuse and harassment. We have in Him a Divine Friend Who truly understands. A quick read of the gospel of John, in particular, demonstrates the extreme patience and perseverance of our Lord under unrelenting verbal attacks and criticism.

Long before Calvary, Jesus bore hateful accusations, sneers, and unjust criticism. Literally no good deed was left unpunished, and Scripture records at least two previous attempts on His life (by stoning, for alleged blasphemy). After one such attack, Jesus heals a blind beggar – unasked – on His way out of town. The man is then excommunicated from the Synagogue for bearing witness to Christ, and Jesus goes out of His way to find him. Jesus sympathizes and is close to the broken-hearted spouses who endure this kind of hurt in a marriage, and realizing this is a key component to healing from the effects of abuse (as we will see in the final section of this book). One of the common ways contempt manifests itself in a marriage that is abusive is through destructive criticism. Let's take a closer look at Proverbs 19:13 for insight into why unchecked criticism is so toxic in all family relationships, and is a form of abuse.

The Continual Dripping of Criticism

Have you ever seen a water-stained drain in an otherwise clean bathtub or sink? Darker than the rest of the porcelain, the ring left around the drain is nearly impossible to remove, no matter how much bleach you use to scrub it. The stain is left from mineral deposits in the water, building up after months (or years) of continual dripping.

Proverbs 19:13 uses this metaphor to describe critical communication: "a wife's quarreling is a continual dripping of rain." Other translations use "complaining", "contentious", or "nagging" in place of "quarreling" – critical speech that is a "continual dripping" because it never seems to stop. This constant criticism or tearing down is certainly not gender-specific behavior; husbands are just as guilty as wives of being verbally abusive (a fact that only The Message seems to acknowledge: "a nagging *spouse* is a leaky faucet"). In marriages with an imbalance of power, it is usually the husband who is verbally berating his wife, the weaker partner.

One of the most common forms of "nagging" or "contention," whether from the male or female spouse, is criticism. In Romans 12:18, Paul issues a very general principle for believers: "If possible, so far as it depends on you, live peaceably with all." This dovetails beautifully with "Above all, love each other deeply, because love covers over a multitude of sins" (1 Peter 4:8). The main medium for getting along with one another (whether within the Church, in marriage, or other relationships) is *verbal communication*, and the Bible has much to say about unedifying speech. Tearing someone down by constantly criticizing them (what they say; what they do; decisions they've made; what they've failed to do; etc.) flies in the face of showing Christ-like love.

When a spouse or child experiences ongoing, relentless criticism, it leaves an indelible stain. Criticism is different from confrontation. *Confrontation* addresses a specific behavior or incident; deals with it biblically; and aims to restore. *Criticism* is rooted in pride (the sense that one is better, or above the one being criticized) and is habitual. It is a fault-finding; never-satisfied pattern of tearing a weaker person down (in particular, one's wife or child). The person who is constantly being criticized can never do anything right. She expects to be criticized for whatever efforts she puts forth, and eventually will stop trying to please her critic because she knows it is futile.

The Spiritual Effects of Being Reviled

James speaks of the tongue as "a world of fire; a world of evil among parts of the body" (James 3:6). Caustic words pierce the soul, because destructive criticism cuts right to the heart of who a person is. Their effect lingers long after bruises heal, and repeated often enough the victim begins to internalize the destructive message. She begins to believe that the words hurled at her like weapons are true, and seeks validation elsewhere.

For example, young women who grow up having their performance, grades, or appearance constantly criticized by their fathers will be seeking male approval by the time they are in their teens. ACBC Fellow Rick Thomas describes this as an "Adamic deficit that sinfully craves approval, significance, acceptance, and affection. [The child of overly-critical parents] has yet to come to the regenerating place of finding those things in God (John 3:7)." He further points out,

> If a person's parenting model consists of bringing critique, mostly in those moments when the child irritates the parent, then their model needs to change. Parenting should not be centered on a parent's pet peeve. The Gospel is so much better than that.[11]

In Marriage

Often, children of critical parents bring criticism's legacy into their marriage – either continuing the cycle of performance-driven, relentless critique and scolding; or, on the other side, the wounds that never healed from being constantly torn down as a child are re-opened by a harsh, overly-critical spouse. This is especially true in the case of women with domineering husbands. She hears the voice of an angry father in the constant dripping of her husband's criticism, and comes to believe that she will never be good enough. Being smashed down by the men who were supposed to love and protect her slowly erodes a woman's confidence, sense of purpose, and relationship with God. Her view of her Heavenly Father is often indelibly stained by the painful words she has internalized most of her life. In her mind, these men speak for God – and the drip, drip, drip of their reproach never seems to end.

Applying the Gospel to the Criticism-Stained Woman

How do we counsel a woman so defeated by criticism who has all but given up on her faith? First of all, it is advisable to start with the very specific

---

[11] http://rickthomas.net/a-biblical-perspective-on-critiquing-children/

habits in her life that genuinely do need to change, to avoid minimizing or glossing over the minor things she can control. But it is crucial to differentiate between *how she performs* and *who she is*. Overcooking the chicken does not mean she is a lazy or careless person; it simply means she accidently burned the chicken. Getting home from work late does not mean she is a selfish person who doesn't care about her family. Deconstructing such accusations, which are indeed abusive, helps make the hurtful statements lose some of their power. She must also be helped to see that not every type of criticism is destructive – is it a specific habit or trait that was addressed? What was the tone and intent of the criticism? Was it delivered in love, with a concern for the well-being of the woman; or a blanket attack on her character?

In an abusive marriage, it will usually be a pattern of the latter. But not every critical husband is an abuser, and it is crucial to understand the difference. There is such a thing as constructive criticism, but women who have grown up being continually nit-picked (particularly by their fathers) are hyper-sensitive to all forms of criticism and cannot "hear" loving concern. They interpret it as an attack, even when it is not.

Next, regardless of age or where she is in her walk with God, the woman crushed by criticism needs to see the Person and Work of Jesus Christ. It is very difficult for a person (male or female) to understand grace if he or she has never experienced it. "My husband can't stand me; God must think the same way about me!" is her line of reasoning. As hard as this is to undo, she needs to be taught (as relentlessly as the critical messages she's internalized) that God is not critical of her. An excellent resource to help women overcome this mindset is Elyse Fitzpatrick's *"Good News for Weary Women"*. She writes:

> ...a serious problem occurs when we start to feel as if our worth is measured by how well we're doing with our to-do lists. And the messages we receive at church, on Facebook, and from the media only perpetuate these unrealistic expectations, creating a relentless cycle of exhaustion and worry. And I have good news for women everywhere: there is hope! God doesn't judge us by our to-do lists. Instead, He calls us to faith in the work Christ has already done. [12]

To a woman bearing the scars of continual criticism, initially the message of God's unconditional love sounds like "just words". She needs to be shown

---

[12] Elyse M. Fitzpatrick, *Good News for Weary Women* (Carol Stream: Tyndale House Publishers, Inc., 2014), 25.

from the Bible, again and again, that there is no condemnation for her. As she continues in the Scriptures, she needs to be taught to deliberately replace the negative things she's been told about herself with the truth of what God says. She needs to recognize who she is in Christ, a dearly beloved daughter of the King, in whom He is well-pleased. The encouragement of another woman to come alongside her (whether as counselor or simply as a friend) is a crucial part of re-wiring her thinking, embracing her true identity, and restoring her joy in Christ.

What is "Gaslighting"?

Another common strategy abusers use to control their victims is called *"gaslighting,"* so-named after the 1944 movie *Gaslight* in which a man manipulates his wife to the point where she believes she is losing her mind. Often referred to simply as "crazy-making," gaslighting is a tactic in which a control-oriented individual makes a victim question his or her reality (or even sanity) in order to gain more power. According to *Psychology Today*, it is a common practice among abusers, dictators, cult leaders and narcissists of all stripes. Gaslighting includes telling blatant lies; denial of statements previously said (even when confronted with proof); attacking what is dearest to the victim and using it against her (in some cases, even her faith); gradually wearing the victim down over time with sarcasm, snide comments, and covert aggression;[13] calculated attempts to confuse their victims about their true motives by occasionally using positive reinforcement; projecting their own faults onto the victim; aligning "allies" against their victim; telling their victim (or others) that she is crazy; and telling their victim that all other people (including sometimes their own family) are liars or are somehow against her. One way in which he seeks to assert control is to convince his victim that she cannot survive without him, and is somehow dependent upon him for 'protection'. This also serves to reinforce fears the woman has about leaving the abuser.

---

[13] In *Character Disturbance*, PhD.-level psychologist and author Dr. George Simon Jr. clarifies the difference between covert aggression, and the often-misused term "passive aggression": "Most of the time I hear people use the term "passive-aggressive" or "passive aggression" what they really mean is "covert aggression." The term "passive-aggressive" is used incorrectly to describe the subtle, hard to detect, but yet deliberate, calculating and underhanded tactics that manipulators and other disturbed characters use to intimidate, control, deceive and abuse others. That's what covert aggression is all about. Although this kind of aggression is often subtle or concealed, there's absolutely nothing "passive" about it. It's very active, albeit veiled aggression." (George K. Simon Jr., *Character Disturbance: The Phenomenon of Our Age* (Marion: Parkhurst Brothers Publishers Inc., 2011), 211.

Stonewalling

Another "punishment" tactic emotionally abusive men often use is known as *stonewalling*, or, as I refer to it, *freezing out*. A controlling man will simply go into full or partial silent-treatment mode for days (sometimes weeks) at a time, put out over some infraction (whether real or imagined) which his spouse has committed. Ignoring a person is a humiliating experience, because it strips her value away and communicates the message that she *doesn't exist*. Refusing to talk or even look at his wife, rather than communicate what the problem is, the stonewaller simply expects her to know what he is glowering about and make amends.

This was a common experience in my marriage, and during the first decade I spent a lot of time apologizing and asking for forgiveness even though I almost never knew what I had done wrong, or what my then-husband was angry about. Over time, his stonewalling ceased to have its desired effect and I would just ignore it. While it would be a stretch to say that I enjoyed being "frozen out," I learned to use the silent-treatment time to focus on my work and children, take up hobbies, and most of all pursue relationships with my friends. Often, communication with my friends was via text and social media as my ex-husband frowned upon my going out to meet them – having a coffee with a girlfriend "t[ook] away from family time."

One Christian blogger who writes about the effects of emotional abuse calls stonewalling "punishment by banishment." While she chooses to remain anonymous online, she writes:

> The silent treatment (feigned apathy; cold-shoulder; silence; distance, and ignoring you) is the worst form of emotional abuse. It is a punishment used by abusers to make you feel unimportant, not valued, not cared about and completely absent from the abuser's thoughts.
>
> It is used as a form of non-physical punishment and control because the abuser mistakenly thinks that if they don't physically harm you then they are not abusers. The truth is, they are far worse at doling out abuse than the physical abuser. Silent treatment is a form of banishing someone from the abuser's existence without the benefit of closure or a good-bye or a chance at reconciliation. In a word … it's meant to torture someone you profess to love.[14]

---

[14] https://suddenlyabandoned.wordpress.com/2013/01/15/silent-treatment-worst-form-of-emotional-abuse/

Isolation

Some abusers attempt to cut their victims off from anyone but themselves and the immediate family. The fewer friends she has, the less likely it is that a woman will receive objective feedback about her predicament. Isolating a woman from friends and family (whether physically, psychologically, or both) serves the dual purpose of keeping her feeling alone and without outside support, and also completely dependent on him. He wants her to think of him as her "savior," and to believe that she will be helpless without him. The less intrusion from the outside, the better. Recently, I read a memoir published in *The Atlantic* by a Filipino man whose family kept a female slave after immigrating to America. They kept her in the house, friendless, uneducated, and undetected for over 30 years. When the man grew up, he felt compassion for the now-elderly woman and wanted to help her go back to her village, but she declined. Having known no other life and frightened even to go to the supermarket, she chose to stay with her captor-family. To a lesser extent, the same dynamic takes place when a husband systematically cuts his wife off from her family, friends and support system as a means of exerting control.

Financial Abuse

Another insidious way abusive men demean their wives (both in marriage and following separation, should it occur) is by controlling or manipulating them financially. Some women, even if they have their own income, are not allowed to spend anything without their husbands' prior permission; are not given any control or say over the family budget; are given an "allowance" (as a small child would be); and/or have to give an account for every penny spent. Because many women have chosen to forgo a career (whether temporarily or permanently) in order to raise children, it's not hard to understand why men have more power economically. This is not a liability, when the two marriage partners are working together and treating one another as equals with different roles, of course. But men who idolize having power over their wives will take every opportunity to control the purse strings as well.

Finances are the number one reason victims can't "just leave" their abusers. Allstate Insurance Company has launched a foundation whose stated purpose is to provide domestic violence survivors the financial skills and tools to break free (and stay free) from abuse. Since 2005, Allstate has helped more than one million women work towards financial independence after escaping their abusers. According to a video they launched to increase awareness of women in this predicament, financial abuse occurs in 99% of all cases of domestic violence.[15] The non-profit organization has trained more than 8,600 service providers to teach financial literacy and asset building programs to domestic violence survivors in all 50 states.

Apart from restricting a women's access to money or keeping her without an income, many women who experience financial abuse hear statements such as:

"How hard is it to stick to an [expletive] budget? You're too stupid to manage money."

"Where do you think you'd live? You'd never survive on your own."

"I cancelled your credit card. Good luck paying for a lawyer when you have no money."

"Let's see how far you can get with no job or money."

Financial abuse is an invisible weapon that keeps victims trapped in abusive relationships.

The high school classmate I quoted in the last chapter told me, "After a six year battle, my divorce finalized in July and he still won't pay a dime. My ex-husband continues to file motions to further destroy me financially." This is, unfortunately, typical of how punitive abusers (of either sex) can become when their victim leaves. And when a woman has been intimidated for years by that control, she often lets this happen. (This is not to say that women are never guilty of financial abuse, or of "using the system" to obtain often-outrageous settlements from their former husbands. There are, of course, many cases of this and unlike the Church, the American probate court system seems somewhat gender-biased towards the woman to the point where "gold-digging" is not uncommon. However, in cases of totalitarian or abusive marriages, women are left more financially vulnerable than men, and it is this liability that many abusive husbands will exploit.)

When "A Fair Deal" Means Signing Everything Over to Him

When I separated from my former husband, I planned to take virtually nothing. In order to spare cost, trauma and embarrassment to our children, I decided not to litigate. Instead, against the advice of several people, I hired an attorney as a mediator. Before meeting the lawyer together, my then-husband had me meet with him alone, where he tried to convince me I ought only to take one seventh of the value of the house (when he would sell it,

---

15   Source: National Network to End Domestic Violence (NNEDV.org)

years in the future) and a couple thousand dollars out of our joint savings account. His rationale was that since I earned less than him, I had less equity in the house. We had been married for twenty years, and I explained that no judge in the world would agree to that. Although the mediating attorney wanted to help me, I allowed myself to be pressured into signing away my rights to alimony, child support, and the marital assets. As a per diem interpreter, I did not have a dime in a pension plan myself yet I did not even touch my ex-husband's $175,000 retirement fund. I actually believed that by being generous to the point of foolishness, he would finally leave me alone and treat me with at least grudging respect.

Of course, I was wrong.

Finally, I hired an attorney to represent me and enforce a court order that had been violated. The lawyer was so horrified by the terms of our Separation Agreement that he also filed a modification so that I would receive child support. My ex-husband was livid. He screamed that he didn't know how I could sleep at night; that American probate laws are unfair, and taunted me for being "lazy" as an able-bodied young adult (I frequently work in excess of 50-hour weeks).

Once in court, my ex-husband's attorney nickel-and-dimed us down to where I agreed to half of the Massachusetts state guidelines for child support for our three younger children. (Even my ex's own lawyer couldn't believe I had signed such a patently unfair Separation Agreement, and he admitted that it never should have been allowed by the judge.) I was content to receive even half of that to which I was entitled. Fortunately, with a solid career (and children well beyond the age of needing daycare), while not wealthy, I at least have a level of financial independence and stability that many women fleeing abusive marriages don't. Millions of women, especially with young children, are working minimum-wage jobs trying to make ends meet. Dependent on food stamps and subsidized housing to survive, I have seen countless women come through the probate court system who are not receiving a dime of support from their abusers. Enforcing a restraining order is easier for the court system than collecting child support or back-alimony, and women continue to suffer this injustice even after their physical safety is ensured. Financial abuse is simply another way of showing a victim who is "in charge".

When Nothing Changes

The ongoing contempt and intimidation of an angry, controlling man who refuses to love her is the soul-crushing reality that so many women within Christian churches endure. The verbal haranguing may play out in a thousand ways. She may be accustomed to frequent outbursts, accusations, and relentless criticism to where she doesn't know who she is anymore. She has tried to speak quietly to her husband. She has spoken to her pastor, who just tells her to go home and try harder to be more "submissive." She has prayed; cried; fasted; called out to the Lord for help – perhaps for decades. No one, save for perhaps her closest friends, knows what she is enduring.

Her husband tells her he will not change; that's just the way he is. After all, he wouldn't have to get so angry if she would just get her act together (and be more 'submissive'). As we saw in the last chapter, the one Bible verse abusive men will often quote is "Wives, submit to your husbands" – the first half of Ephesians 5:22. At times, she despairs and flees the house so he will not see her tears....and mock her further for her "weakness" or "emotionalism." She self-flagellates for messing up – yet again. She has heard that she is incompetent, or self-centered, or lazy so many times that she begins to believe that she really is as worthless as he implies – which makes her want to hide from God.

A woman enduring emotional abuse feels completely isolated. She desperately needs someone to step in – an even higher authority than her husband – and affirm that she is not alone; she is not unloved; and there is nothing that she could have done biblically to deserve this treatment. As tragic as it is, there are times when the marriage cannot be saved. While some branches of evangelicalism hold that abuse never constitutes biblical grounds for divorce, where an abusive man remains stubbornly unrepentant Scripture indicates otherwise. Divorce is an incredibly painful, life-altering decision. Many women have been brow-beaten into staying in abusive marriages with unrepentant husbands by another half-verse, "God hates divorce" (Malachi 2:16), without regard for the rest of the verse (His condemnation on husbands who treat their wives treacherously) or consideration of a more important biblical principle: God hates *abuse* even more.

Sadly, all too often the abuser refuses to change (or is incapable of change, not recognizing the reason for his own behavior). When the marriage covenant has been broken through ongoing abuse, trust is shattered. Try as they might, well-meaning clergy cannot always put the pieces back together again, nor should the victim feel compelled to return when the situation has not changed. Churches that take an absolute stance against divorce in cases of abuse (including battery, and even adultery at times) are not faithful to the whole of Scripture. Broken women now must endure the added burden of being shamed by the churches they trusted to protect them – all in the name of saving a *marriage* over a *person*. In the next chapter, we will look at the biblical argument for when abuse is legitimate grounds for divorce.

CHAPTER 3

Is Abuse Ever Biblical Grounds for Divorce?

"Domestic abuse is a test case for your theology. Eminent people may have great theology in many areas, but if they don't get it about domestic abuse and divorce, they are gravely in error (in my humble opinion) and need to sit down and seriously examine their doctrine. Until they do, victims of abuse will continue to be unbelievably hurt by the church. God is not happy about this! I suspect He would like to spit them all out of His mouth for their lukewarmness when it comes to protecting the vulnerable (who are mostly women and children)."
– Barbara Roberts, author of Not Under Bondage: Biblical Divorce *for Abuse, Adultery and Desertion*

By the time a Christian woman is even contemplating the horrifying thought that her marriage may be beyond repair, she has endured so much for so long that she has given up hope that anything will ever change. She (and her children) may be in physical danger, and need to get to safety. Her husband may be a habitual adulterer, who shows no signs of repentance. Or, it may be a less physically-dangerous but equally toxic form of torment – years of unrelenting verbal abuse that have driven her to despair.

While a full treatment of when divorce may be biblically-justified is beyond the scope of this book, some discussion of the matter is in order because of the erroneous assertion that many contemporary churches take: namely, that domestic abuse is never grounds for divorce. Abused women who are living with the covenant-breaking spouse are often chided (and even blackmailed with the threat of excommunication) if they do file for divorce, even after they have made repeated attempts to salvage the marriage. This dogmatic stance is a misrepresentation of God's high view of marriage, and puts the blame for sin squarely on the victim's shoulders – rather than on the unrepentant abuser, where it belongs. Unpacking what Scripture says about such situations is necessary, in order to shed light on an unfortunate situation many abused Christian women find themselves in.

One excellent book on this subject is Pastor Hugh Vander Lugt's booklet, *God's Protection of Women: When Abuse is Worse than Divorce*. As the senior research editor for RBC (now Our Daily Bread Ministries), Lugt's 1982 book is a concise, yet exegetically-rich resource which biblically challenges the contention that divorce is never justified by abuse. Far from being a plea to reason based on emotionalism (or even pastoral experience), Lugt effectively shows how a faulty hermeneutic has led many conservative pastors and churches to teach that Matthew 5:32 is the final and definitive word on divorce.

Just as there is sinless anger (Ephesians 4:26), there is also sinless initiation of divorce. God cannot sin, yet He actively initiated disciplinary divorce (Jerimiah 3:8). Until and unless there is fruit of repentance (Matthew 3), and evidence of love (John 8:31ff, cf. v. 42), those who claim to be children of Abraham are not automatically included in the New Covenant (Romans 11). One Boston-area pastor wrote to me, "If a wife seeks the support of church leaders and the husband is unable or unwilling to change his patterns of verbal abuse, I think it is incumbent upon those church leaders to regard him as an unbeliever. That follows the instructions Jesus gave in Matthew 18:15 – 17. Divorce is then a regrettable but valid option...it is regretful that church elders also very often do not recognize the more vulnerable position the woman is in [with a domineering husband]. Perhaps this is also because of a belief that "headship" in marriage means that a husband's "authority" rests in his person *per se*, irrespective of his own obedience to Jesus. Many others, including myself, view that as highly contested, to say the least. I have already argued that "headship" in marriage is only true authority to the extent that a husband is faithful to Jesus, so that he is not a "head" by virtue of simply being a husband. The question is, what kind of husband is he being?"

Linguistic Misconceptions

In the thorny endeavor to unpack all of what Scripture has to say about divorce (as well as abandonment and abuse of different kinds and re-marriage), it is dangerous to conclude that one verse contains the full and final answer on the permanence view of marriage. Moses, Jesus and Paul all recognized a range of marital conditions that are worse than divorce.

Historically, although women were often treated as property, the Puritans were a notable exception when it came to recognizing the seriousness of marital abuse:

> In the spirit of the Reformation, Puritans didn't see marriage as an indissoluble sacrament but as a civil contract that could be terminated if either party did not fulfill fundamental duties of marriage. Although cruelty was not a recognized ground for divorce in the Puritan era, there are those who thought cruelty to a wife was a type of desertion. [16]

In his discussion of marital abuse, Lugt demonstrates how, even in modern times, women have been overly-subjugated by a misunderstanding of the word "helper" in Genesis 2:18.

> There is no sense in which this word connotes a position of inferiority or subordinate status. The word "suitable for" literally means "in front of", signifying one who stands face to face with another, qualitatively the same, his essential equal, and therefore his "correspondent" ("Hard Sayings of the Bible, pp. 666-7, IVP, Downers Grove, 1996). [17]

Sixteen times in the Bible the Hebrew term *ezer kenegdo* is used in reference to a person, and fifteen of those are in reference to God as our "warrior helper." The sixteenth is used in Genesis 2 in reference to woman, that she is man's "warrior helper" (*Ezer* means "help" and *kenegdo* means "partner"). God created women to be 'warrior helpers' to their men.

Another fallacy that many writers have pointed out is that male domination is a "right" inherited from the Fall. However, if we are consistent to the rest of Genesis 3, it was a *curse* that, like sickness, thorns and discord, should be resisted and fought. With sin, these maladies entered what was previously a perfect and harmonious world, with idyllic relationships. The tendency to dominate, dictate and abuse is a perversion of the Creation order that has no justification in Scripture.

A Bulgarian proverb states: "Better a horrible ending, than a horror without end." To state that God wills His daughters to stay in destructive, toxic or dangerous relationships (not merely disappointing ones) contradicts everything we see scripturally about His loving and protective character. One abuse survivor, who asked to remain anonymous, put it this way: "I upheld

---

[16] Hugh V. Lugt, *God's Protection of Women: When Abuse is Worse than Divorce* (Grand Rapids: RBC Ministries, 1982), 4.

[17] IBID, 6.

my wedding vow. I'm not someone who would ever leave a marriage or break a promise. I would never knowingly allow violence or abuse to break up my family. I would never knowingly let sin take root in my home. I wouldn't put my children through the trauma. So I had no choice but to leave my husband."

Mosaic Law

Even the most weak and vulnerable women in Hebraic society – daughters or wives sold as slaves or concubines – were protected under the Law of Moses. Quite progressive for its time, Exodus 21:7-11 lists the "three foundations of marital duty" – namely, the provision of food, clothing, and 'marriage rights' – often interpreted as affection and marital love. (In fact, the Jewish Ketubah lays these out as a *contract*, not unlike Ephesians 4.) Breaking these conditions is, in fact, a violation of the marriage covenant. But more significantly, it shows the *principle of protection* that is seen throughout Scripture, from the lesser to the greater: *if God would provide protection and care even for a slave, how much more is owed to a free wife?*

Exodus 21:11 makes it clear that if the husband fails to fulfill this contractual obligation, he is to "let her go free". This has been proven conclusively by theologians to mean a formal divorce, the *'get'*. Of course, neither rabbis nor Christian pastors argue that this is the ideal; rather, the Mosaic divorce allowance was given by God for humanitarian means – to protect women from cruelty. Deuteronomy 21:10-14 similarly makes provision for the divorce, protection, and remarriage of non-Israelite prisoners of war.

As Laura Petherbridge writes,

> It takes two to get married, and only one to break the vow. Stop placing both spouses under one sin. (This is normally the wife. In twenty-five years I've *never* had one husband tell me his church abandoned him when the wife walked out, but I've lost count of the hundreds of women who have wept over the shunning of a church when her husband left.) Just because a sin has occurred don't assume both have sinned.[18]

Unraveling Malachi 2:16

Scripture reveals an ongoing intent of protection first by Moses, (whose Law Jesus upheld completely during His ministry); then subsequently by

---

[18] http://www.ibelieve.com/relationships/this-is-the-reason-god-actually-hates-divorce.html

the prophet Malachi, whose words were intended to protect women being wrongly divorced by their husbands; and finally by Jesus, in His indictment of the Pharisees. One of the most frequently misquoted verses in the Bible regarding divorce is Malachi 2:16:

"For the man who does not love his wife but divorces her, says the Lord, the God of Israel, covers his garment with violence, says the Lord of hosts. So guard yourselves in your spirit, and do not be faithless." (ESV).

In *Not Under Bondage: Biblical Divorce for Abuse, Adultery and Desertion*, Barbara Roberts addresses the correct etymology of that passage. The verse is often incorrectly and incompletely translated as "I hate divorce" and used as a catch-all conversation stopper to assert that divorce is never permitted biblically. However, this is not the intention of the passage (written during a time period when male casual divorce was rampant). She writes:

> The incorrect translation came about as follows. The word "hates" in Malachi 2:16 is *he* hates. The Hebrew denotes third person masculine singular = he. The King James version had "For the LORD, the God of Israel, saith that he hateth putting away." Many subsequent translations switched the third person "he" to a first person "I" without any grammatical warrant. For example, the 1984 NIV was " 'I hate divorce,' says the Lord God of Israel." Possibly translators thought the switch was okay because it retained the sense of the KJV — that God feels the hatred [for divorce]. They did not seem to worry that "I hate divorce" was grammatically inaccurate to the original Hebrew.

> But modern translations are starting to correctly this mistake. The construction in Hebrew ("he hates... he covers") shows that the one who feels the hatred is not God, but the divorcing husband. To be faithful to the Hebrew, the verse could be rendered, "If he hates and divorces," says the Lord God of Israel, "he covers his garment with violence." It is talking about a husband who hates his wife and divorces her because of his aversion for her. Therefore, Malachi 2:16 is only referring to a specific type of divorce: divorce for aversion, which could be dubbed "hatred divorce". Divorce for hatred is treacherous divorce: if a man hates his wife and dismisses, he "covers his garment with violence" — his conduct is reprehensible, he has blood on his hands.[19]

---

[19] https://cryingoutforjustice.com/2013/10/24/god-hates-divorce-not-always/ Barbara's book can be purchased at notunderbondage.com or from any book retailer.

Biblical scholar Joe Sprinkle also has pointed out that the context of Malachi 2:16 is a limited one: taken in accordance with the allowances for divorce made elsewhere in Scripture, it is clearly only certain divorces in certain circumstances to which God is opposed. While upholding the sanctity of marriage, we can see how the New Testament teaching on divorce demonstrates how Christ, Moses and Paul's teachings complement one another.

New Testament Application

Even a superficial reading of the gospels reveals that Jesus demonstrated a concern and caring for women that went beyond the social mores of the First Century. And it is plain that the God of Scripture is a Protector and Defender of the weak and downtrodden. So then, does Matthew 5:31-32 over-ride the provision offered divorced women in Deuteronomy? Did Jesus completely nullify the Mosaic Law of protection with this one verse?

"It was also said, 'Whoever divorces his wife, let him give her a certificate of divorce.' But I say to you that everyone who divorces his wife, except on the ground of sexual immorality, makes her commit adultery, and whoever marries a divorced woman commits adultery." (Matthew 5:31-32, ESV)

Of course not. Just as with all of Scripture, a correct hermeneutic demands we examine context (Literal-Historical and Synthetic Principle of Scriptural interpretation). Jesus was, in the Sermon on the Mount, addressing the Pharisees' specific excesses and "stretches" in interpreting and teaching the Law of Moses. They had added hundreds of laws onto the original Levitical code, and the abuse of the divorce clause in Deuteronomy 24 was no exception. In reality, divorced women of the First Century were disgraced and had few career prospects outside of prostitution. It is not biblically consistent to say that He was contradicting the conditions Moses had set, but is more consistent with the passage that He was forcing the Pharisees to focus on the condition of their own hearts. Relational sin was the point; the one statement was clearly not intended to be the single and final word on divorce (as Paul later demonstrates).

Later in Matthew 19:3-9, Lugt notes, we in fact see the Pharisees trying to entrap Jesus by confronting Him with the Law of Moses on the same subject. While upholding the sacred ideal of the permanence of marriage, Jesus did not disagree with Moses in allowing divorce.

Commenting on the allowance made for hardness of heart, Dr. Willard notes: 'No doubt what was foremost in His [Jesus'] mind was the fact that the woman could quite well wind up dead, or brutally abused, if the man could not "dump" her. It is still so today, of course. Such is our "hardness of heart". Better, then, that a divorce occur than a life be made unbearable. Jesus does nothing to retract this principle…no one regards a divorce as something to be chosen for its own sake…but of course a brutal marriage is not a good thing either, and we must resist any attempt to classify divorce as a special, irredeemable form of wickedness. It is not. It is sometimes the right thing to do, everything considered.[20]

The Mosaic Code and the teachings of Christ on divorce complemented each other. Jesus was forcing the hypocritical religious leaders of the time to examine their own hard hearts in putting women in danger (both by abuse and neglect, and unrighteous divorce), as they were actually ignoring Moses' rabbinical provision for women. There was no need for Jesus to cite all of these scripturally-valid grounds for divorce, any more than He explained the full Gospel of salvation by faith alone when speaking to the Rich Young Ruler. *Context* is crucial. During his indictment of the Pharisees, Jesus was not addressing women in distress. He was addressing the self-righteous men who did as they pleased in "putting away" their wives.

Of course, Jesus also didn't mention the additional circumstances meriting divorce later cited by Paul in 1 Corinthians 7:10-11: "To the married I give this charge (not I, but the Lord): the wife should not separate from her husband (but if she does, she should remain unmarried or else be reconciled to her husband), and the husband should not divorce his wife."

Note that neither of these chapters (Matthew 19 or 1 Corinthians 7) gives a full litany or examination of all of the circumstances under which a woman might be justified in seeking a divorce from a covenant-breaking husband. Also, as Paul would have been well-acquainted with Mosaic teaching on re-marriage, why the no-remarriage clause? Lugt argues that the context of chapter 7 suggests Paul was answering specific questions raised by the Corinthian believers about celibacy (advocated by some even within marriage), and about marriage itself. He urges wives not to leave, but as a concession states that they are then to remain unmarried. Nowhere do we see the Early Church pressuring divorced women to "reconcile" with their husbands (under any circumstances) or to stay with abusive men. In fact, both the epistles of Peter and Paul speak directly to the men and command caring and love towards "the weaker vessel" – an extremely progressive command in the First Century!

---

[20] Professor Dallas Willard, *The Divine Conspiracy*, (New York: HarperCollins, 1997), 169-70.

Furthermore, Paul clearly rebukes the church at Corinth for tolerating men who were revilers (1 Corinthians 5:11). They are the ones to be removed from church fellowship; not their victims. Pastor Sam Powell asks a rhetorical question of those who refuse to concede that abuse is, biblically, grounds for divorce:

> How can we refuse to allow divorce from a reviler... when the scripture forbids us from even eating with a so-called brother who is a reviler? Doesn't this involve us in hopeless contradiction? You force his wife and children to live with him. "He didn't leave any bruises. You aren't really in danger. You have no grounds for divorce."
>
> Are you willing to excommunicate the victim for obeying the command of the Lord in this passage? Or is it your contention that she should still continue the intimacy of marriage, but perhaps eat separately? I'm having a hard time understanding this position.
>
> Perhaps this is why the [local] church today has become so corrupted. We have been tolerating corrupt leaven. I say it is time we stop, and start obeying the Lord. You can be a reviler, or you can be a Christian. You can't be both. In fact, according to this text, a reviler who calls himself a brother is far, far worse than an outright unbeliever. A reviler who is allowed to call himself a brother will corrupt the whole church.[21]

Mako Nagasawa, a former campus director with The Navigators and biblical scholar, explains how the Levitical Code and New Testament application complement each other. He writes,

> The important question for Christians is how Jesus and Paul interpreted this Old Testament law of divorce for neglect and abuse. One problem the Church has grappled with for centuries is that Jesus appeared to forbid divorce "for any cause ... except sexual immorality" (Matthew 19:3-9). The common interpretation until recently has been that Jesus allowed divorce only for adultery. This has been very difficult to understand pastorally and seems absurdly contradictory of other biblical principles since it appears to condone abuse and abandonment. Even as early as AD 200 the Church Father Origen was puzzled by it. He said that if a wife was trying to poison her husband, or if she deliberately killed their baby,

---

[21] https://myonlycomfort.com/2017/06/02/christians-who-revile/

then for her husband "to endure sins of such heinousness which seem to be worse than adultery or fornication, will appear to be irrational." (Origen, Commentary on Matthew II.14.24) Nevertheless, Jesus' teaching appeared plain, so the Church followed it."

But recent research into Jewish documents show that discussions about Exodus 21:10 – 11 and Deuteronomy 21:1 – 4 were separate discussions. So the discussion between the Pharisees and Jesus about Deuteronomy 21 were isolated to that text:

"This mystery has been recently solved by research in ancient Jewish documents where we find that the phrase 'Any Cause' divorce was a legal term equivalent to the modern no-fault divorce (see the chapter 'No-fault Divorce'). By means of a legalistic interpretation of the phrase "cause of immorality" in Deuteronomy 24:1, some rabbis allowed divorce for both 'Immorality' and 'Any Cause'. When they asked Jesus what He thought, He confirmed that this phrase referred merely to divorce for adultery (nothing "except sexual immorality"). He totally rejected the newly invented divorce for 'Any Cause'. The misunderstanding through the centuries has been the belief that Jesus was referring to all grounds for divorce rather than the 'Any Cause' divorce specifically."[22]

But what bearing did this discussion about Deuteronomy 24 have on the criteria given by Exodus 21? Did Jesus categorically overrule Exodus 21? No. Jesus actually said nothing about the law of divorce for neglect and abuse in Exodus 21. This was partly because He wasn't asked about it and partly because it wasn't a topic of debate like the text in Deuteronomy 24. All rabbis still accepted these biblical grounds of neglect of food, clothing and love and ancient Jewish marriage contracts found in caves near the Dead Sea show that its three requirements were incorporated into Jewish marriage vows. Every couple would promise each other to provide "food, clothing and bed" (a euphemism for sexual intercourse), just as it says in Exodus 21.[23]

---

[22] David Instone-Brewer, "Marital Abuse," *BeThinking*, 2012. http://www. bethinking.org/bible/bible-scandals/5-marital-abuse

[23] Mako Nagasawa, personal correspondence with author.

The "Separation…but No Divorce" Position

Although in the Greco-Roman context separation constituted a legal divorce, some churches currently claim that they protect women by "allowing for separation for a time," which they base on 1 Corinthians 7:10-11 without looking at the full context of the letter. They insist that the ultimate goal must be reconciliation (essentially under any circumstances), ignoring the possibility that the woman may choose to remain single or that the man's sin pattern may justify (and even necessitate) divorce. While well-intentioned, the insistence on only a temporary separation is problematic and rarely solves the root issue. "Crying Out for Justice" blogger "Jeff S." writes:

The two biggest problems with "you can separate but not divorce" are:

a) It's not a biblical solution. How can we be in a "marriage" doing all the things we are called to if we are separated? Yes, there are probably times a separation, mutually decided, can help with healing; but the way it's advocated for in abuse situations reads more like a technical "married but not married" so everyone can feel good about the way they've parsed the law and found a loophole.

b) Separation with an eye on reconciliation has built in pressure to reconcile, which is very dangerous for someone who has had their boundaries repeatedly violated and likely is not good at setting them up (or keeping them up). The last thing you want to do when someone needs to learn to erect healthy boundaries is to keep asking them when they are going to take them down.

Martin Luther, John Calvin, Origen and a number of other Early Church Fathers upheld that abuse in certain cases could constitute biblical grounds for divorce, and maintained that Jesus did not nullify the Mosaic Laws on divorce and remarriage. It is a relatively modern interpretation held by many Reformed and conservative evangelical pastors that divorce is never allowable in cases of abuse, including verbal. Luther, in particular, was quite adamant that continual conflict, hatred, and cruelty were what drove the believing spouse away, and as the marriage covenant was thus broken, were legitimate causes for divorce.

It is crucial for pastors, counselors and others in Christian ministry to understand God's original design for marriage, as well as His protection in certain circumstances where divorce is allowed as a concession. Untold amounts of needless guilt and victim-shaming has occurred in the name of "being faithful to the Word", when the Word really has much to say about cruelty. Marriage is indeed a covenant, and sadly, once the marriage covenant has been thus violated, the abuse survivor is not obligated to stay.

Examining the *context* and *hermeneutic* in which certain passages were written is illuminating in dispelling the "abuse is not biblical grounds for divorce" fallacy. This didactic belief serves to keep women in bondage. Marriage was created for people; not the other way around. When marriage becomes an idol for its own sake, and women are coerced into staying in (emotionally, physically, or spiritually) destructive situations to save face for the Church, God's Word and intent has been misunderstood and misrepresented.

The Lysa TerKeust Travesty

During the writing of this book, well-known Christian author and president of Proverbs 31 Ministries Lysa TerKeurst filed for divorce from her husband after years of his infidelity and substance abuse. In a public statement, she wrote:

> My husband, life partner and father of my children, Art TerKeurst, has been repeatedly unfaithful to me with a woman he met online, bringing an end to our marriage of almost 25 years. For the past couple of years, his life has sadly been defined by his affection for this other woman and substance abuse. I don't share this to harm or embarrass him, but to help explain why I have decided to separate from him and pursue a divorce. God has now revealed to me that I have done all I can do and I must release him to the Savior.
>
> Anyone who knows me and Proverbs 31 Ministries knows how seriously I take marriage. I've always encouraged women to fight for their marriages and to do everything possible to save them when they come under threat. So, for the past couple of years I have been in the hardest battle of my life trying to save my marriage...I believe I have the capacity to love Art and to forgive him, but his steadfast refusal to end the infidelity has led me to make the hardest decision of my life. After much prayer and consultation with wise, biblically-minded people, I have decided that Art has abandoned our marriage.[24]

The backlash against Lysa (rather than her adulterous ex-husband) from some leaders in the evangelical community was astounding. Jeff Maples, the

---

[24] http://lysaterkeurst.com/2017/06/rejection-heartache-and-a-faithful-god/

editor of "Pulpit & Pen" (a well-known Reformed blog) wrote: "We will be praying for repentance for Lysa TerKeurst to turn from her rebellion against God and walk in righteousness in accordance with His statutes as found in Scripture alone." Then, in an even worse indictment, a number of Christian media outlets insisted that she step down from ministry and specifically leadership of Proverbs 31, on the grounds that her divorce now disqualified her.

Black Christian News (BCNN1) editors wrote:

> No one with any spiritual discernment is going to buy that her husband is the big, evil, bad monster and she's the sweet, little lamb. Whenever there is a divorce, both parties have issues. Sadly, many Christians have bought into this lie that it is always the man causing the problems in the marriage and that the woman is always innocent. And that is just not the case.
>
> No one is condemning you, but you need to admit that you were not perfect in your marriage either, and we urge you to reconcile with your husband. As you stated in your blog post, you 'always encouraged women to fight for their marriages and to do everything possible to save them when they come under threat.' We urge you to do the same. As the reason for continuing your ministry, you stated that you were determined "not to let darkness win." Well, the way you do that is by not letting darkness win over your family by reconciling with your husband and getting your family back together.[25]

Art's ongoing infidelity, which is a very serious form of abuse, was proven. By all accounts he refused to abandon his affair and return to a monogamous marriage. Although Lysa stated that she had forgiven him many times for the adultery and substance abuse, he continued to return to it and would not give up either vice. She had single-handedly fought for the marriage for a quarter century, and now the very ministry leaders with whom she served God were throwing her under the bus for pursuing a very biblical divorce. Notice the victim-blaming in the editors' castigation of her – they directly state that since she was not 'perfect', she must share in the blame for her ex-husband's philandering and addiction.

Much like the claim that abuse victims must share in part of the blame for their mistreatment, this extreme patriarchal thinking absurdly places the sole responsibility for saving the marriage on the woman's shoulders. And

[25] http://blackchristiannews.com/2017/06/lysa-terkeurst-we-love-you-but-you-need-to-resign-from-proverbs-31-ministries/

Lysa *had* embraced more of that responsibility than was ever hers to bear – not only by fulfilling her end of the marriage covenant, but also through forgiveness and her long-suffering attempting to gently "win her husband over" and bring him back to the truth. She cannot be blamed for his failure, nor can she be criticized for taking the final step that Scripture instructs spouses to do in such situations. There is a serious problem in the Church when leaders insist that even clear-cut, black-and-white cases of biblical grounds for divorce are sinful...on the part of the victimized spouse.

In the next chapter, we will look at some of the ways scriptures have been misconstrued and have thus conditioned Christian women to accept emotional abuse as "headship" or "spiritual leadership". We will examine some of the teachings prevalent in conservative evangelicalism, and how they enable patriarchal thinking to grow and ultimately enable abusive men.

CHAPTER 4

Conditioning and False Guilt

"When a Christian woman is convinced that there is redemptive value in crucifixion, she will not only find "contentment" in what should be intolerable circumstances but find spiritual meaning and divine purpose in her own and her family's suffering. This sort of mental gymnastics can easily manifest as a form of Stockholm Syndrome when victims believe that they have no options or way out. They delude themselves into feeling they do have a certain amount of control when they "choose" to embrace, support and defend their captor. It is oddly empowering to a trapped person to say, "This is what I want. Yes, it may be painful, but it is actually beneficial to my spiritual growth."
– Vyckie Garrison, author of No Longer Quivering

Why does a woman stay in an abusive relationship? It's an often-asked question, both by people of faith and non-believers. Particularly when the abuse is physical, it is mind-boggling that a woman will stay with (and even defend) her abuser. Yet as directors of battered women's shelters attest, even after having bones broken and eyes blackened, countless women will voluntarily return to their abusers, even risking their lives to do so.

Battering is an extreme (although common) example of spousal abuse, for which law enforcement should be brought in immediately. It should be self-evident that such behavior is not only unbiblical and a breach of the marriage covenant; it is criminal. Bystanders should intervene if the woman will not help herself. However, my purpose in this book is to focus more on the subtler forms of abuse which are non-physical. There is an epidemic among women in parts of the Church who faithfully keep the "code of silence" about their suffering. The teaching of some movements and popular leaders of Christianity serve to condition women to accept emotional abuse as legitimate "biblical headship" or "spiritual leadership". While most Christian men (certainly the vast majority) are truly loving their wives and providing humble and gentle leadership of their families, the culture of patriarchy (male-as-superior) serves to enable men with abusive and controlling tendencies.

Avoiding Labels

Writing this chapter will be particularly challenging, because I want to avoid the over-use of labels or terms which may mean different things to different people. Also, within certain movements/theological camps there are variances of belief. For example, it is impossible to talk about the broad "Patriarchy" movement in specifics, as there is a spectrum of belief and practice even among those who would consider themselves "patriarcha." The Family Integrated Church movement, for example, which is a subset of the broader patriarchal movement, has on their website a list of "FIC doctrines," including the belief that young women should not go on to college (they are only to be "keepers at home", confined to domestic duties exclusively) and an ecclesiology that puts all men in charge of the Lord's Supper at worship services. However, not every church that considers itself "Family Integrated" (nor every individual adherent therein) necessarily subscribes to all of the "official" views. Unlike Roman Catholicism, which is completely homogenous across every nation, diocese and parish under Vatican rule, conservative evangelicalism has so much variance and nuance in their views (including on women's roles) that if we are to identify the source of false teaching, we must very carefully define our terms.

One pair of terms which deserves attention at the outset is *"complementarian"* versus *"egalitarian."* I realize that as a woman writing a book about misogyny and abuse (often veiled by the Church as righteous submission or "suffering for Christ"), I run the risk of being labeled a "feminist." Let me say from the outset that I do not consider myself as such, at least by the way the term is commonly used by society today. If by "feminist" one means simply that women are equal to men (including their husbands) spiritually, intellectually, morally, and judicially, and equally deserving of fair treatment and privilege, I would accept the term. Yet "feminist" is considered a pejorative by Bible-believing Christians, and perhaps for good reason when we see the extremes to which the modern feminist movement has gone. Following the election of President Trump, I watched in disbelief as raving, hysterical young women shouted obscenities and decried "the patriarchy." My reaction, as someone who had come out of a high-control patriarchal religious group was "You gals don't even know the *meaning* of the word 'patriarchy!'"

The theological construct that says women are subservient or inferior to men is one that we have already seen is unbiblical. Now, let's turn to the two schools of thought on local church leadership (which overflow into the home). Complementarians believe that while men and women are equal before God, we each have different callings, gifts and roles. Part of this "different but equal" belief is that God's design of male authority in the New Testament Church is permanent. Women, although we may serve in ministry in most ways, are precluded from the church offices of pastor, elder and deacon.

Egalitarians, by contrast, don't simply believe that men and women are equal (as the name suggests); but believe that women are allowed to preach; teach; pastor churches; and fill any other ministry role traditionally held by men. The practice of "mutual submission" (which frankly seems to work better in democratic societies) versus the man having the final say in family decisions is a natural extension of the view of complete equality in role and ministry.

"Complementarian" Does Not Equal "Abuse"

Although I will probably lose a significant proportion of the readers of this book by saying so, I still consider myself largely in the complementarian camp. It is not complementarian belief that I see as unbiblical; it is the *distortion* of it that I find abhorrent. While it seems illogical that we would take the command of 1 Corinthians 14 (cited in chapter 1) to mean complete silence by women at all times within a church building, I do see enough passages alluding to male headship in the local church to assume it is God's permanent pattern for ecclesiastic leadership. And we do see husbands in the role of protector and primary provider (although many passages, including Proverbs 31, indicate that women may also run businesses), so it is not difficult for me to reconcile equality of men and women with men being in the governing role of the local church. This is certainly not to say that women cannot or should not use their spiritual gifts in the Church, or contribute freely to decision-making and theological discussions. She is not to be literally "silenced" within the four sanctuary walls.

While I do not subscribe to Roman Catholic doctrine or ecclesiology, the complementarian understanding of men leading the Church (priests are all male because the Apostles were all male; and because of the words of Paul prohibiting women teaching in the local church) without delegating women to second-class status in the home or workplace seems to me a correct application of this challenging dichotomy. I know of no Catholic women who have ever been forced to homeschool their children or been forbidden to work outside the home in the name of Titus 2; nor does emotional and spiritual abuse seem to be as rampant in their communities. While I am not advocating much of Catholic doctrine, there seems to be a form of complementarianism within the Church itself co-existing with a practical egalitarianism in the home.

Even though I may still call myself a complementarian, let's make it clear that abuse of power, rule by fear/intimidation, and angry demands for "submission" are *not* God's design for a harmonious family – nor a Christ-honoring church. I am truly appalled to see this full-blown authoritarian attitude and behavior covertly justified in the name of complementarianism. Sharon Hambrick, an attorney and Christian writer, commented on social media: "Patriarchy will be as abusive and demeaning to women as it can get away with. Women will be as close to property as they can get away with, as close to legal nonentities, as powerless, as voiceless, as invisible as they can get away with. Only the civil law constrains them."

How on earth did we get here in conservative Protestantism?

How Some Christian Writing Degrades Women

In looking at 1 Peter 3:7 and its instruction that husbands should honor their wives as weaker vessels, "Council for Biblical Manhood and Womanhood" editor and communications director Greg Gibson claims that weaker means "of great value". He then tells men how to properly evaluate their women:

> Men, think about your most important possession and how you treat and honor it. Now triple your efforts and apply that same carefulness in how you treat and honor your wife... Remember, she is the weaker vessel–an *object* of intense value. ("Building a Marriage Culture – husbands, honor your wives", emphasis mine.)

Blogger Tim Fall comments:

> There you have it, men. The way to treat your wife right is to look on her as one of your possessions. The most prized (three whole times more valuable than your car or boat!) but still a possession.
>
> Women are objects.
>
> The objectification of women is a theme in patriarchy. And this is not some outlier among CBMW's writings. The article has been promoted on social media by CBMW's president and other leaders of the organization. Spreading this language of objectification leads to people thinking of women as objects; that's how language works.

Why do patriarchists do this? Why do they say they are honoring a person and then objectify the person as a possession?

It's because they don't understand people the way God does. [26]

Another popular website, "Biblical Gender Roles," despite its innocuous-sounding name, literally reads like a primer on how to abuse one's wife. In a recent post, "7 Ways to Discipline Your Wife," a writer (using the pseudonym "Larry Solomon" as he will not reveal his true identity) advocates punishing one's wife like a child for such "sins" as watching TV too often; over-spending; and declining his sexual advances. He even states directly "I do not believe wife spanking is necessarily a sin." In his first paragraph, he claims that marriage is not a partnership, but rather "a Patriarchy." (This post was simply one of many which twists Scripture in order to degrade and demean women.) Such writing feeds into the egos of men with anger and/or control issues, as well as abuser-enabling pastors.

Our Own Worst Enemies

We Christian women are conditioned by what we read and hear, and we eagerly buy books and go to retreats and conferences because we earnestly want to learn how to please God. While numerous male Christian writers and teachers have written many things dismissive of women (especially their feelings, emotions, goals and use of their gifts), some of the most damaging messages Christian women absorb come from other women. Unfortunately, I have attended conferences in which certain "workshops" essentially primed women to accept emotional abuse. One such lecture, given by a well-known female speaker at a nouthetic counseling conference, put the onus on a woman and her choice of words and demeanor for her husband's sinful anger. The last thing a woman with a chronically-angry husband needs to hear is that his sin is somehow her fault.

Many "tips", books and seminars in the conservative evangelical world seem to center around just being better, more submissive wives in order *to lead our husbands closer to God*. If a woman speaks her mind, she is brow-beaten. If she is in a truly difficult marriage, she will blame herself. Why shouldn't she? Her mentors – these seemingly-perfect Christian teachers with their lives in order and their lipstick perfectly applied – are telling her that if she just tried harder; trusted God more; prayed more; accepted her suffering better – her marriage would become "God's best." The man is never the problem. If she allows herself to think that his sin is destroying the

---

[26] https://timfall.wordpress.com/2015/07/06/patriarchy-when-husbands-possess-wives/

marriage, she must be "bitter." She is most certainly "rebellious." This is the message largely being fed to women at such conferences.

Author and abuse survivor advocate Natalie Herbranson has also noted the problem of women perpetuating the very lies that keep their sisters in bondage. On her blog, "Visionary Womanhood," she writes:

> I've commented before that it has been my experience that it is women who do the most false teaching in this matter. I cannot tell you how many times I have been chastised by women for not being as submissive as I should be. Truth is, they were 100% right, but their brand of submission never seemed godly to me because it allowed their husbands to continue in their sin decade after decade. It tends to be the women who don't quite know what to do with my less-than-traditional attitude. I don't think that the role women have played in the perpetuation of this should be overlooked.
>
> We believe a lie if we think that a married woman's husband is the equivalent of God to her. God lets her know what He (God) wants when her husband lets her know what he (the husband) wants? Sorry, but that's man-worship, plain and simple. Worshiping a man is not spiritual or healthy.[27]

Books that drive this "gospel" of sanctified misogyny are so numerous they should have their own sub-genre in the "Women's Interests" section of Christian bookstores. Debi Pearl, for example, in *Created to be His Help Meet*[28], has written that women should defer to their husbands to the point of never having an independent thought, and complimenting him for the sole purpose of "building him up." She writes:

> Never demand a man love and cherish you because he ought to. (31)
>
> Your husband will be selfish, he will be unkind....not respect your rights...foolish....cruel....actually walk in sin...... (55)
>
> In most marriages the strife is not because the man is cruel or evil; it is because he expects obedience, honor and reverence and is not getting it. Thus he reacts badly. (79)
>
> If some worthless men had wives who were more _____, you fill in the blank, they would not be so worthless. (278)

---

[27] https://emotionalabusesurvivor.com/the-role-of-women-in-their-own-destruction/

[28] Debi Pearl, *Created To Be His Helpmeet: Discover How God Can Make your Marriage Glorious* (Pleasantville: No Greater Joy Ministries, 2004), 31-278.

Throughout her book, Debi blames women for their husbands' sin, then exhorts them to accept this abuse as a "rewarding yoke" (76) lest they "run back to mama and sleep in a cold bed living off of food stamps" (111). She also claims that the "Commanding" man reflects part of God's nature (75), and as such, is part of His will for the woman:

> Command men.....are known for expecting their wives to wait on them hand and foot.....She is on call every minute of her day. Her man wants to know where she is, what she is doing and why she is doing it. He corrects her without thought. For better or for worse it is his nature to control...... A woman married to a Command Man wears a heavier yoke than most women but it can be a very rewarding yoke....her walk....is easier because there is never any possibility of her being in control.... Command men have less tolerance so they will often walk off and leave their clamoring wife before she has a chance to realize that she is even close to losing her marriage... The Command man feels it is his duty and responsibility to lead people and he does whether...they want him to or not. (77-78)

This book was sold and endorsed by the church that I had no choice but to leave following my divorce. Is it any wonder that women in abusive marriages were held in such low regard there?

With more subtlety than Debi Pearl, in *Lies Young Women Believe*, unmarried (i.e., at the time of the writing of the book) Nancy Leigh DeMoss indicates that women should not be career-oriented, or see any professional pursuit as superior to the "higher calling" of marriage and motherhood. Of course marriage and motherhood are wonderful and fulfilling; God created them to be! But He also gave girls and women unique gifts, intelligence and talents to develop.

Another female writer in the Christian blogosphere, Lori Alexander, tells wives both on her blog "The Transformed Wife" and Facebook page of the same name that they were created for their husbands' enjoyment; that women who have been sexually assaulted are "self-centered" and "defrauding their husbands" if they do not enjoy sexual relations with them; and should simply "try harder." She also chides wives for such infractions as snacking in front of the TV, and for having any expectations on him in the marital relationship (which, in her view, is not a partnership but a hierarchy). This position has no biblical support whatsoever, even if one appeals to the Old Testament.

Voddie Baucham, a well-known celebrity pastor, spoke at a conference several years ago on biblically-prescribed gender roles and categorically claimed that women who pursue careers are outside of God's will (i.e., sinning). His entire message was based on Titus 2:5, but he did not touch on the fact that the home can be "kept" by delegating some responsibilities, as the Proverbs 31 woman did. He cited an encounter he'd had with two female students at a Christian university who challenged his view. A law student and a medical student, they insisted they would be as good at motherhood as they would be at their perspective careers. "No you won't," Baucham rebutted. "The average physician or attorney works 60 hours per week. You will not be raising your children; you will be paying someone else to raise them."

While Baucham's point had some validity – most careers *do* demand long days and on-call status – it was his black-and-white thinking (and painting all career women everywhere as "outside of God's will") that was wrong. There is no biblical prohibition on women seeking higher education or working outside the home (Lydia, the Macedonian businesswomen and Christian convert, is only one example of an Early Church working woman).

"Biblical Womanhood"

"Biblical womanhood" is an ambiguous catch-phrase which has gained popularity in recent years, often subjectively interpreted to mean "stay-at-home, homeschooling mom who sews and bakes." Recently, I came across an online magazine called *Keepers at Home*. Dedicated to the idea that holy = cooking/sewing/cleaning, the site sells a Little Keepers at Home handbook "so that girls ages *4 to 6*, can begin to be little keepers and future Christian homemakers!" (Emphasis mine) Really? Do we really want to send our daughters the message that being a follower of Jesus essentially means cooking well and doing craft projects? Of course, some women love homeschooling their children, baking, and teaching Sunday school – and are good at it. These are great activities, and women who enjoy them should be encouraged. But so should the women who don't.

I am certainly not arguing that women should seek to usurp their husbands, or fill a man's role. But what is often instilled in evangelical women is that their gifts and abilities should be channeled *only* into homemaking, and to seek to use them elsewhere does not honor God. This leads to needless guilt, which comes out both in the counseling room and in private. For a woman with a college degree such limitations can be devastating – she may even be made to feel guilty for having a career. Using the fine mind God has given her is a way of glorifying Him; and women need to be told this. The world needs more Christian women in medicine; in the hard sciences; and in other fields. Far from being unbiblical, God is greatly honored when His daughters work up to their highest potential. A woman can serve God with joy if she is doing what she loves; and if she loves computer science more than doing crafts at women's conferences, she has the freedom in Christ to pursue it.

What Christian women need to realize is that following Christ does not limit them strictly to homemaking duties, but rather frees them to embrace the unique gifts, abilities and calling He has placed on their lives. *Biblical womanhood means a woman, heart sold out to her King, pursuing the life He ordained for her and her alone to live.* It means cultivating the passions and talents He has uniquely gifted her with. It means being a leader like Deborah; a businesswoman like Lydia; an instructor of her children like Lois and Eunice; and being actively engaged in charitable work like Dorcas. It can mean staying home and teaching her children full-time, if that's her calling; it can mean becoming a nuclear physicist or isolating the cancer genome if that is the passion God has instilled in her heart. Just as there are "many members of the Body" (1 Cor. 12:12), there are many individual versions of womanhood that fall well within God's blessing.[29]

Setting the Stage for Abusive Relationships

Another Christian writer posted a list of "do's and don'ts" on Facebook, telling women how to have a successful marriage: not to expect their husbands to help with housework; meet *any* of their needs except to economically provide for the family; and to simply try to "make his life as easy as possible". What most caught my attention, however, was a portion of the quote which was underlined: *"Expectations destroy relationships."*

This is exactly the sort of advice targeted towards Christian wives that sets them up for emotional abuse (or at the very least, an emotionally-distant husband unable to connect with his wife as an equal). It is not about the housework, or a division of labor based on traditional gender roles. That is an individual arrangement that can be decided by couples based on preference. If a husband does not feel it is his role to give the baby a bath, fine. If she does not want to mow the lawn or snowplow the driveway, that is reasonable. However, as another reader pointed out, the quote seemed to imply that a woman who is honestly overwhelmed is sinning if she asks for help. She is *not*.

Many women fall into serious depression because they are overwhelmed by the demands of running a household (often while homeschooling children)

---

[29] Excerpt from article written by author, originally published as "Biblical Womanhood: Breaking Molds and Building Each Other Up", *Biblical Counseling for Women* (blog of Reigning Grace Counseling Center)

and are made to feel guilty if they expect assistance from their husbands (Remember Andrea Yates?). Would we tell men they are wrong to expect their wives to cook their dinner? Iron their shirts? Meet their sexual needs? It would be hard to find a male writer willing to take this stance.

Even so, household chores are not the main issue I had with the quote. *It is the notion that in a relationship, it is wrong to have any expectations on the other person.* And, the additional burdens we put on ourselves to stay in God's good graces are unnecessary.

Expectations Are Healthy and God-Ordained

The Bible sets forth some very clear expectations for both husbands *and* wives, which we have already looked at. Negating some or all of them for the purpose of "building up" one party in the marriage (the husband) to the exclusion of the other (the wife) puts a huge imbalance of power in place. Telling women "You won't have a happy marriage if you expect anything from your husband" is dangerous for at least three reasons. First, it demeans men. A godly man seeks to honor and obey God by loving, serving, protecting, encouraging, comforting and helping his wife. He is the spiritual leader in the home, and is the one to whom his children look to see an example of Christ. It is rather condescending (if not insulting) to tell women to "expect nothing" of them. Secondly, it saddles Christian women with the responsibility for their husbands' happiness, and additional guilt if they fall short. These women are often already burdened by self-recrimination, trying to live up to their own standards of perfection, and usually blame themselves for their husbands' short-comings. The last thing they need is to be rebuked for having "expectations".

Lastly, telling women to have zero expectations in the marriage relationship opens the door to abuse. As any relationship expert will tell you, it is impossible to have a mutually-satisfying and respectful relationship between two adults if they are on unequal footing. When one is subordinate to the other to this extent, it leads to one of the single biggest catalysts of spousal abuse: *entitlement.* Lundy Bancroft writes,

> *Entitlement* is the abuser's belief that he has a special status and that it provides him with exclusive rights and privileges that do not apply to his partner. The attitudes that drive abuse can largely be summarized by this one word. [30]

---

[30] Lundy Bancroft, *Why Does He Do That? Inside the Minds of Angry and Controlling Men* (New York: G.P. Putnam's Sons, 2002), 52.

Bancroft then goes on to describe how men's and women's rights within the family are the same size – with each having equal rights to having their opinions and desires respected, as well as input into decision making and the right to live free from physical and verbal abuse. He then diagrams how in the family of an abuser, (who feels thus entitled), the women and children's rights are substantially diminished while his are inflated. This is a picture of life in patriarchal families. (While I am not implying that all such families are abusive, this inflation of the man's "rights" at the expense of his spouse's certainly sets the stage for abuse to be rationalized.)

The 'Umbrella' of Authority

One proponent of patriarchal authoritarianism was Bill Gothard, who in 1961 founded The Institute in Basic Life Principles (IBLP). IBLP was a seminar ministry of sorts, which promoted homeschooling, large families, and purported to teach pastoral counseling. Much of his teaching on counseling had a heavy victim-shaming slant, particularly his materials on counseling victims of sexual abuse. "Unwise choices" and sin were assumed to be the root reason for every problem in an individual's life.

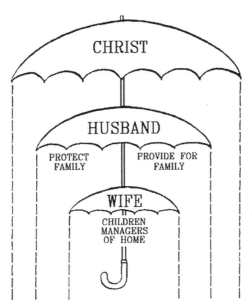

Gothard developed a diagram to symbolize male authority using three umbrellas: the inner-most one representing the wife, swallowed up by a larger umbrella representing the husband; over which the largest umbrella represented God. He termed it the "umbrella of protection" and claimed it represented the biblical principle of authority, but in fact such an image is anything but biblical. Nowhere does Scripture teach that a woman must be "covered" by her husband lest she be outside of God's protection or provision. Despite the clear scriptural teaching that men and women are equal in God's eyes, the diagram implies visually that a woman does not have direct access to the Lord and is essentially only a possession – of her husband. This harmful "umbrella of authority" diagram became very popular among conservative Christian groups, and was often used in marriage studies.

In 2014, Gothard was disqualified from ministry because of sexual abuse allegations and stepped down. It was only then that theologians and church leaders called on the Board of IBLP to evaluate the harmful doctrines promoted by this group, and linked this repressive authoritarian teaching to the "moral failings" of Gothard and other IBLP leaders.

Vision Forum

Another organization that conditioned women to accept an inferior status was Vision Forum. The now-defunct group advocated many aspects of the patriarchy movement, including "shepherding"[31], homeschooling, "Quiverfull" beliefs, and women's roles being restricted to the house and family. Vision Forum even went so far as to list their own "Tenets of Biblical Patriarchy" on their website, which included the following assertion: "Since the woman was created as a helper to her husband, as the bearer of children, and as a "keeper at home," the God-ordained and proper sphere of dominion for a wife is the household and that which is connected with the home." Much like the nation of Gilead in the dystopian novel *The Handmaid's Tale*, working outside the home or having a career was considered sinful even for college-educated women.

A huge market existed for Vision Forum conferences and books among Bible-believing Christians who were desperate to promote family values. Don and Joy Veinot of Midwest Christian Outreach interpreted the Vision

[31] The "Shepherding" movement (also called "Discipleship Movement") grew out of the charismatic movement of the 1970's and '80's, and created a hierarchy of submission and authority which does not appear in Scripture. The movement heavily influenced many groups and churches with its unbiblical emphasis on submission to authority, and has been criticized for its cult-like manipulation and intimidation tactics. Beginning as "Christian Growth Ministries" in Florida, the movement originated the idea of "spiritual covering" which they felt could only occur under the "protection" of authoritarian church leadership. This stands in stark contrast to Ephesians 5:23, which instructs believers to look to Christ directly for guidance, protection and provision. Many churches have taken the recent practice of "discipleship" to unbiblical ends, as well.

Forum statement to imply that "women really cannot be trusted as decision makers" and "unless a daughter marries, she functionally remains pretty much the *property* of the father until he dies." In 2013, Vision Forum was shut down by its board of directors after its president, Doug Philips, was sued for sexual abuse. Their website has since been removed from the Internet, and is only viewable through the Wikipedia archived link. Yet their teachings continue to proliferate among Christians who subscribe to extreme patriarchal interpretations of authority, leaving women without a voice and being made more vulnerable to both spiritual and spousal abuse.

Redemptive Value in Suffering?

Besides a rigid understanding of gender roles and a belief in absolute male authority, one teaching common to all these "ministries" is that women should embrace suffering "for the sake of righteousness." 1 Peter is an epistle often mentioned to women seeking relief from abuse, as chapter 4 alludes to the believer's suffering for doing good. However, what is often overlooked in such counsel is that while suffering may be part of God's will for the believer, in abusive situations the suffering is caused by the sin of another person. Letting sin go unchecked – or worse, enabling it by unbiblical teaching – is never part of God's will. Twisting the first six verses of chapter four to keep women in abusive marriages is, in itself, spiritual abuse. The woman now believes that God has put her into a situation from which there is no escape. In this paradigm, it is His will for her to be tormented by her husband, and if she resists, *she* is now the one in sin.

While trials in the life of a believer are part of our sanctification, suffering in and of itself does not purify anyone. Christ's suffering on our behalf is all the sacrifice needed for redemption – it is the height of hubris to think that suffering, for its own sake, makes anyone more holy. One of the most harmful effects of emotional abuse in a marriage is that since a wife has been groomed to see her husband as an absolute authority figure, if he is angry or disgusted with her she implicitly feels that God must be, too. Just as a child's view of God can be distorted by having an angry, volatile father, she projects her husband's unfavorable view of her onto God. Far from sanctifying her, ongoing marital abuse can deeply damage a wife's relationship with God. Being told this is "His will for her" will cause her to distrust the God to Whom she should run for comfort.

Vyckie Garrison writes,

> The more a Christian woman cares and the harder she tries to
> live according to biblical principles for 'godly womanhood', the

more she, her husband, and their children suffer. These women who take "biblical family values" to their logical extremes are phenomenally strong, and are single-mindedly determined to follow God's path no matter how difficult and painful the journey may become.

Stretch the meager grocery budget so you'll have money left to buy homeschool curriculum for half a dozen kids? Sure, no problem! Clip coupons, learn to barter, garden and raise chickens and rabbits, sew your own diapers and menstrual cloths, teach the kids to dumpster dive, "repurpose" absolutely everything? That's easy! Cook three meals a day from scratch to feed a dozen for less than $150 per week? It's tricky, but doable! *The Lord provides!* Push your body beyond endurance with perpetual pregnancy, childbirth and breastfeeding? *"I can do all things through Christ who strengthens me!"* Home school, home business, practice hospitality by home churching, *and* keep up with the mountains of laundry? Quiverfull moms are masters of delegation. Cut yourself off from all support systems of mom, sisters, even fellow church women to protect your family from their compromising "feminist" influence? *Well yeah, because Jesus is with me always and the Holy Spirit is my comforter.* Love and submit to an overbearing, controlling husband? Quiverfull wives yield *with grace*.[32]

This expectation to be "perfect" is a form of works-righteousness. This is a classic example of the 'heavy burdens' Jesus mentioned being placed on His children's shoulders in Luke 11:46. When a woman cannot live up to the impossibly high standard put on her, she feels the added burden of failure. It is through the suffering of Christ on her behalf that she is redeemed; not through her own perfectionistic attempts to be the 'perfect Christian wife'. If patriarchy was God's perfect plan for humanity, then God would not have deemed "men ruling over women" as a consequence of sin (Genesis 3:16). The Gospel reverses all of sin's curses; hence it is "good news" for women.

Certainly, not all (or even most) men who subscribe to the absolute male-headship theological view are abusive. In a patriarchal environment, men are taught that they are the sole providers and protectors of their wives. Most take their call to love and cherish their wives very seriously. It would be unfair to suggest that men or even churches who subscribe to patriarchy are, by nature, abusers. They are primarily seeking to obey and honor God,

---

[32] http://www.alternet.org/my-conservative-christian-nightmare-i-spent-16-years-abusive-religious-sect

and sincerely believe that their model is the biblical one. Yet a relationship in which one person is seen as inherently weaker (or lower) than the other can never attain true intimacy. When taken to their logical conclusion, the teachings of patriarchal authoritarianism groom men to become dictators, and condition women to accept abuse as God's will.

In the next chapter, we'll see through the eyes of a male victim of spousal abuse how this teaching of redemptive value in suffering does not only wound women, but also Christian men who experience marital abuse.

CHAPTER 5

When Dying to Self Leads to a Crushed Spirit

"I will serve my Creator in the light, but I will not
serve an abuser in the darkness."
– A male abuse survivor speaks up

Jeff S., a regular contributor to the blog "Crying Out for Justice," endured years of verbal abuse in his first marriage. His church contributed to the problem by refusing to validate the pain Jeff was going through, and communicating that neither he nor his feelings mattered. He says, "There are two very important things with regard to gender. One is that abuse happens both ways. But, the other is that in our culture men have inherent power. So, the net of those two things is that while abuse goes both ways, it isn't the *same*."

During the writing of this book, I also heard from an ordained pastor here in New England who had himself endured years of psychological abuse from his former wife. Although asking me not to share his story publically, he did affirm that abuse happens to men – and members of his church turned on him (spreading gossip, shunning him) as well. I was surprised to hear that a well-respected man who had endured so much would also become the victim of secondary spiritual abuse, but men do also suffer from mistreatment within the Church.

Verbal torment is denounced in the Bible, regardless of the offending party's gender. Because most of this book addresses abuse inflicted on wives within Christian environments, I asked Jeff to write this chapter to show how men are also affected by abuse. While the level of intimidation may not be equal to a woman being mistreated by her husband, some churches apply the same fallacious reasoning that domestic abuse "brings glory to God" to men's experience.

This following is one man's perspective:

When I chose to divorce, at the time I felt very alone, and that how I was treated by my church was as an outlier. What I came to realize after listening to countless stories of abuse victims, mostly women, was that not only was I one among many, but that many others had it much, much worse. And this started with one important factor: I was believed.

I have since learned that women can often experience a disbelief from others that their well-regarded husband could do the things they reported. It's an uphill battle just to get someone to even listen to her. I cannot say for sure that it was because I was a man that I never had to prove myself, but I know that I never had to convince anyone that the way my wife treated me was awful.

This should have made things easier on me, and yes, I at least had the dignity of being believed. However, this belief came with its own dark side, which was that I was told that the abuse didn't matter – it was my lot in life. That is a pretty painful thing to hear in its own right. Compared to being disbelieved, this is the flip side of the emotional coin, and neither option is great. Either you are not believable or you are a punching bag. This led me to question my identity and relationship to God at a very core level.

My Identity

When I understood that the church was okay with the pain I was experiencing, it led to a real crisis of identity. To have someone see you in pain and affirm it as good is soul-destroying.

The following is a portion of a song I wrote (and later recorded):

> Does it matter who I am?
> They told me it was OK
> That the way that I was made to be should all be wiped away
> I tried to lose that part of me
> And swallow my desire for peace
> But I never overcame the hope that one day I might be free

I spent *years* trying to get to a place where anything that was me was wiped away. Because what was *me* was hurting and in pain. I kept thinking that my goal in the Christian life was to get rid of "me" and replace it with Christ. That sanctification was all about replacing myself with Jesus. And while *I* hurt in the marriage, Jesus wouldn't.

People would say that's crazy. Why would I think that? But, it isn't an unreasonable thought, especially for someone who is struggling with his sense of identity. The modern church uses a great deal of language that supports this horrible view. Our songs and sermons talk about replacing the self with Christ and so on. I realize that this language isn't intended to convey a message of totally destroying oneself, but when you aren't healthy, an extreme message can be inferred. But to top it off, a lot of modern worship music and style also supports the idea of "losing yourself." People go to an "out of mind" place where they sway to the music and appear to transcend themselves. There can be the notion of getting consumed by Christ.

I remember one line in an otherwise good song by Hillsong: *"Rid me of myself, I belong to You."* We have to be very careful what we teach when our worship and messages seem to indicate that the goal of the Christian life is to lose our identities, because it isn't. And when I wrote the lyric *"Does it matter who I am?"* above, this was a real question I asked myself and wrestled with, not just a dramatic question to open a song. Because modern Christianity can easily be interpreted to mean that no; it doesn't matter who we are.

When the Church is willing to accept abuse, it sends a message to abuse victims that they are not important, but real Christianity is a different message: God has made each of us to be who we are, and He is intently interested in us as individuals, unique and special. I finally got to a place that I understood that, but it took a lot of healing.

Abuse or Divine Suffering?

Another struggle that being believed caused me was understanding the will of God for me. My church told me that the point of my pain was to glorify God and my situation was "no different from missionaries being martyred for the faith."

Wow, really?

I tried to believe that. I really tried. I tried to believe that there was some God-magnifying, truth-proclaiming, soul-saving reason for me to suffer. But that isn't the reality, is it? Did anyone look at my situation and go, "Wow, I get it – Jesus came to save me from my sins. Let me repent and be saved!" I did ask the elders at my church what the goal was – what was I trying to show the world? They never could give me a concrete answer except "to display God's truth to the world". What truth? The truth that we have the power to endure anything? Shouldn't the cause of our need for endurance matter?

The real "truth" that we display to the world by accepting abuse in a marriage is that God would have us suffer for someone else's pleasure (not

His). Because that is the goal of abusers – for the victims to suffer for their pleasure.

Sure, those who persecuted the believers in the New Testament enjoyed the power and control they wielded when trying to intimidate the Church, but the believers were being persecuted because they were sharing the Gospel. So what was the great goal of my suffering, the goal so noble that the Church could call me to it in good conscience?

The next lines of the song I recounted above talked about this facet of my struggle:

> How I could let all that I was be emptied and destroyed
> A sacrifice to bring no hope, just one more broken toy

A broken toy. *When they call us to suffering, they are calling us to feed an abuser's sense of entitlement and lust for power.* They are saying God created us with a specific purpose: to be a plaything for someone else. Not to spread the Gospel. Not to worship Him – but to be a toy. It is sick.

I cannot accept that when God knit me together in the womb, that this was why He did it. No, we were not created to be toys for abusers – to suffer and feed their need for power and control. We were created to live in the light and proclaim the Gospel. We were created to glorify God and to enjoy Him forever. I will serve my Creator in the light, but I will not serve an abuser in the darkness.

Wanting Love; Not "Grace"

As I moved on from the church that handled my divorce so poorly, I encountered a wide variety of reactions from others. One of the maddening things I heard a lot from well-meaning Christians was that there was grace for me in my divorce. Even this struck at the idea of my identity, because a person in need of grace is a person who has transgressed. Someone who, just for wanting to be at peace has failed God. I wanted to tell people "I don't want grace, I want love."

To say "I don't want grace" is not to mean that grace is unnecessary in the overarching sense of my faith. I *need* grace. I depend on grace. Every moment of every day is only possible because of grace. The statement "I don't want grace, I want love" was about my divorce specifically. And what did I mean by that? I mean, I do not believe that divorce is something that I need or want people (or God) to "overlook" or to "deal with." It's not something that requires people to summon up their most gracious feelings to extend to me. It's something that was necessary, and as painful as it was, I am comfortable with it being a part of my life. I am comfortable with my decision, and I believe strongly that God is comfortable with it too. In fact, my faith depends on it.

I remember clearly when a well-meaning Christian told me "The great thing is, even if you were wrong in your divorce, there is grace to cover that." I completely understand the point this person was trying to make and why he thought it was encouraging. He wants me to look forward in confidence and not be hindered by my past. What he does not understand is how my experience translates that statement. What I hear is, "The great thing is, even if God hated you enough to pin you down while you were being hurt and hold you in place with a 'high view' of marriage, he can overlook you wriggling out from his death-grip."

Many people fail to understand that the view that God's law is violated by divorce in circumstances of extraordinary pain (neglect, abuse, adultery, abandonment) is a view that God hates us. I'm sure they would deny this. I'm sure if John Piper were sitting here right now talking to me he would insist that God does not hate me at all, even after I divorced. He is graciously open handed on the issue (so open handed that he could get along with his own church that takes a different view). In fact, I had a good friend tell me we could "agree to disagree" on the issue of divorce. By while for him this seemed a gracious compromise, it struck my heart deeply and painfully and we will never be as close again.

I cannot "agree to disagree," nor can I accept that I might require "grace" to cover the divorce (though I certainly cling to grace for every sin I committed in my marriage; I will not claim to have been a perfect husband). I simply cannot accept that God would hold me in my marriage and subject me to that intense pain at the hand of my ex-wife. That makes me an object of God's hatred, at odds with the core of my faith that God loves me.

To accept even the possibility that my divorce was a sin is to accept the possibility that the foundation of my faith is a lie. Even grace, the great distinguishing doctrine of Christianity, flows from God's love. We only get grace from God because He loves us. Permanence doctrine is not a secondary issue to me; it strikes at the core. If I do not have God's love, how can I have His grace?

I hope that in time the Christian community can develop a better empathy for those who are abused and/or divorced and stop offering us "grace." The church should affirm that God loves us and that He was not okay with our pain. If our lives bear fruit and we are genuine believers, it is safe to trust that we fought hard for our marriages and held them in a very high view. If we are trusted in this way, no one needs to worry about whether or not we require grace or whether we were to blame. You need only love us and show us the love of Jesus.

This would mean that those like me who divorced to get away from abusive spouses wouldn't have to fear vulnerability with fellow Christians, knowing that we are always one potential step away from hearing another person imply that God hates us. It would mean the Body of Christ could be a safe place for us, something many of us didn't feel at the lowest points when we needed the Church the most.

The final part of the song I wrote about my struggle with my identity and how God views me was not a request for grace for my guilt, but rather a declaration of His good plan, that He cared about me, and that I could trust His work in my life. This is what I believe compassionate Christianity tells abuse victims, that God cares for and loves us:

> *Your strong voice calls out to me and tells me I'm forever Yours*
> *That You love me and You know me, and You gave me life forevermore*
> *You want me to be loved*
> *You want me to be free*
> *You created me to be who I am*
> *And You are in control.*

CHAPTER 6

Why is the Church a Refuge – for Abusers?

*"For certain people have crept in unnoticed who long ago
were designated for this condemnation, ungodly people, who
pervert the grace of our God into sensuality and deny our
only Master and Lord, Jesus Christ."*
– (Jude 1:4)

Boz Tchividjian, founder of GRACE (Godly Response to Abuse in the
Christian Environment) and grandson of Billy Graham writes, "Offenders
are experts at twisting the truth, minimizing abuse, — and exploiting guilt
in order to create a fictional narrative that paints themselves as the victim of
those who confront them about their injustice."[33]

The Abuser-friendly Environment in Churches

Imagine a micro-culture in which a closed group operates as a law unto
itself. Where clandestine meetings, agenda-laced correspondence and leaders
pre-disposed to believe a man's version of events over a woman's have the
power to shun, excommunicate, or "discipline" at will. Where members
of this sub-culture who have served faithfully within its ranks for decades
now find themselves pariahs – their reputations damaged; their children
indoctrinated in misogyny; their sanity questioned. Their crime? Standing
up for themselves and refusing to endure further abuse (either marital,
spiritual or both).

Although I had been a part of the evangelical sub-culture for 25 years, until
I went through it myself I had no idea how common the tactic of victim-

---

[33] http://religionnews.com/2015/05/15/a-grand-deception-the-successful-response-
of-sex-offenders/

shaming, downplaying the serious (and often irreversible) nature of abuse and excommunicating women who flee abusers is. Incredulous at what I was experiencing, I started to do research....and didn't have to look far. Women from the same church where I was being pressured to "reconcile" with my former husband (notwithstanding no terms of repentance ever being met) started calling, emailing and texting me that they had had similar experiences at our former church.

We were not alone – many books and survivors' websites reveal how widespread this phenomenon is within certain branches of Christianity. I was shocked. Testimony after testimony of women in 21st century America demonstrated that misogyny and a culture of silence surrounding spousal abuse is alive and well. Where does this come from? Why are conservative evangelical churches havens for abusive and controlling men? Why, when the entire counsel of Scripture shows God as a Protector and Defender of the weak, is it so commonly the *woman* who is put under duress for exposing or fleeing her abuser? As we saw in chapter 3, even the Mosaic marriage covenant, progressive for its time, guaranteed basic rights to wives – those wedded in slavery, as well as the freeborn. Does it not seem counter-intuitive, then, that the abused women are held up to castigation, while their abusers remain in good graces within their churches? Yet this happens, over and over again; all across the country.

Repentance Leads to Change

One part of the reason for this dichotomy between orthodoxy and orthopraxy is that churches of a certain theological stripe hold a very superficial view of *repentance*. When you break it down, they seem to believe that if the abuser is simply "confronted" and told he is in sin, he will automatically agree; say "I repent"; and change will be forthcoming. They base this view on an over-simplified understanding of God's sovereignty: "God can change anyone." Taken at face value, those four words are true. However, when we leave it there, that statement allows abusers to circumvent any personal responsibility, and the assumption is always that God *will* change the abuser's heart (no matter how many years the abuser has proven otherwise). To have this statement thrown at you, as the spouse of an unrepentant abuser who has stated repeatedly that *he* is not the problem and *will not* change, is the equivalent of being backed into a corner, tied to a chair, and having duct tape placed over your eyes and mouth.

This begs the question: Can abusers change? Experts Barbara Roberts and Jeff Crippen answer that concisely and correctly on their blog, "Crying Out for Justice":

To say that abusers cannot change removes responsibility for sin. They can change, but the vast majority choose not to, which is what the experts state. When God punishes them, their punishment is just. Abusers have options for treatment and are accountable. Once the marriage covenant is broken through abuse, the abused partner does not need to stay in the marriage waiting for the abuser to change. The abuser's recovery is a separate issue and his change is his own responsibility, not his wife's. This is the mistake most churches make. These churches have over-sentimentalized marriage and are legalists.[34]

We need to pause here and robustly affirm that because of the finished work of Christ on the cross, anyone can change through the indwelling power of the Holy Spirit. The angriest man alive may become a completely new creation (2 Corinthians 5:17). To claim otherwise undermines the power of the Gospel. Saul, on the road to Damascus, was en route not only to abuse but to *slaughter* believers, and was dramatically and irrevocably changed by an encounter with the living Christ. Abusers can change, if they have a relationship with Christ and desire to "put off" their old nature, which includes anger, rage, malice, slander and obscene language (Colossians 3:8).

Turning Black into White

The problem is that when abusers are confronted about their behavior, not only will they often lie outright to their pastors and/or counselors, they will spin events and hateful, hurtful statements they have made in such a way as to minimize or project blame onto the other party(ies). (We will discuss in more detail how abusers minimize and deny their behavior in the next chapter.) Abusers are often extremely intelligent, master manipulators who can use their skills to generate an appearance of change, however temporarily. Frequently, Proverbs 18:17 is pulled out as a rationale for minimizing the victim's experience: "The one who states his case first seems right, until the other comes and examines him." Unfortunately, this has been the experience of many, *many* of us women who have made the difficult choice to confide details of their abuse to our pastors.

Abusive men will also often claim to their pastors that their wives are the ones abusing them. Psychologists have noted that the inherent sense of entitlement that controlling men carry causes them to mentally reverse aggression and self-defense (see fuller discussion of reactive abuse in next chapter). If the woman expresses herself at all, they consider it "abuse".

---

[34] https://cryingoutforjustice.com/

Within patriarchal authoritarian circles, it will not be hard at all for the man to find supporters of this view. After all, the abuser's favorite verse is Ephesians 5:22: "Wives, submit to your husbands."

I experienced this accusation firsthand from my former husband, who loved to bring up the fact I had concealed an eating disorder from him decades earlier as proof I was "abusing" him and "not submissive enough." As a woman in my twenties and early thirties, I did indeed have a problem with bulimia that I was terrified to tell him about. I concealed it from him out of shame and fear of what he would say or do to me if he knew. God did grant me repentance, and seven years after completely recovering I shared my testimony of healing with him. Rather than rejoicing that I had been delivered, he was furious that I had hidden my shameful secret from him and asked rhetorically, "What should I do? Should I kick you out of the house?" Following the divorce, he used this example to the pastor, our children, and anyone else who would listen of what a deceitful, horrible wife I had been.

Many churches, especially of the Reformed evangelical variety, seem predisposed to believe the man. Women who complain of abuse, especially absent obvious physical evidence, are almost universally assumed to be lying. Even when the pastor claims (at least initially) to believe her account, it is not uncommon for the abuser to sway his perception of what actually happened and even enlist the counselor as an ally. The wife, who has usually endured years (or decades) of torment and humiliation in silence, is now cast as "unforgiving" and having "hardened her heart." Nothing could be further from the truth. The abused woman desperately wants to be able to forgive (and reconcile, if separated from her husband), but she first needs to be able to see the fruit of a changed heart in his life. She needs assurance that things will finally change.

Unfortunately, they rarely do.

Indicators of an Unregenerate Heart

Sometimes, counselors view abusers with truly depraved (evil) hearts as ordinary sinners who simply mess up. An unregenerate (although oftentimes professing Christian) with an evil heart will twist the facts, mislead, lie, avoid taking responsibility, deny reality, make up stories, and withhold information. "Evil hearts," says abuse expert Leslie Vernick, "are experts at fooling others with their smooth speech and flattering words. But if you look at the fruit of their lives or the follow through of their words, you will find no real evidence of godly growth or change. It's all smoke and mirrors. Evil hearts crave and demand control, and their highest authority is their own

Common Characteristics of Abusers

- Blows up at small incidents
- Excessively jealous
- Insecure, with poor self-image
- Blaming others
- Manipulative and controlling
- Issues with alcohol and/or drugs
- Family history of violence
- Makes threats of violence, breaking or striking objects
- Cruel to animals and/or children

- Uses physical force
- Uses verbal threats
- May have rigid stereotypes of gender roles
- Gets involved in relationships quickly
- Acts out instead of talking
- Uses "playful" force during sex
- Is intentionally cruel and degrading
- Moody and unpredictable

If you need help call the National Domestic Violence Hotline: 1-800-799-7233

Infographic by Saludify.com

self-reference. They reject feedback, real accountability, and make up their own rules to live by. They use Scripture to their own advantage but ignore and reject passages that might require self-correction and repentance."[35]

Abusers demand grace for themselves, but are utterly unable or unwilling to give it to other people (often possessing a perfectionistic mindset). Lacking empathy, the abusive man typically has no real intention of making amends to the one(s) he has harmed. They lack remorse, while masquerading as having a noble character.

All these traits make it difficult for a counselor to discern when he is dealing with a truly evil heart, rather than a struggling brother. Further complicating the issue is that abusive men are so adept at "playing the game" that they

---

[35] https://christiancounseling.com/blog/counseling/five-indicators-of-an-evil-and-wicked-heart-1/

may easily portray themselves as superb, loving fathers to their churches and community, (including on social media), and even ingratiate themselves to their children so much that the wives they abused do not seem credible. I have counseled several women who have experienced this. Their façade is so convincing that no one believes the abusive man could possibly be anything but the "wonderful Christian father" they pretend to be.

What's Your Motivation?

Abusive men can and have been known to change their behavior and heart attitudes, if their motivation is strong enough. Lundy Bancroft, the foremost recognized expert on the minds of abusive and controlling men, writes:

> There are no shortcuts to change, no magical overnight transformations, no easy ways out. Change is difficult, uncomfortable work. My job as a counselor is to dive into the elaborate tangle that makes up an abuser's thinking and assist the man to untie the knots. The project is not hopeless – if the man is willing to work hard – but it is complex and painstaking. For him, remaining abusive is in many ways easier than stepping out of his pattern. Yet there are some men who decide to dig down inside of themselves, root out the values that drive their abusive behavior, and develop a truly new way of interacting with a female partner. The challenge for an abused woman is to learn how to tell whether her partner is serious about overcoming his abusiveness. [36]

While Bancroft is not a Christian, his writing on abuse is excellent because it calls angry and abusive men to account for their behavior and forces them to take responsibility. There is no hint of psycho-babble or rationalizing abuse as a "sickness" with him. Bancroft seeks in his counseling model to unmask the deeper issues driving abusive behavior (for example, recognizing that the reward for abuse is *control*, not sadistically causing pain for its own sake) and working with men to deliberately and intentionally dismantle their worldview of personal entitlement. This is refreshingly different (and frankly more biblically sound!) than the all-too-common practice in churches of putting the onus on the woman for reconciliation at all costs, regardless of whether her abuser is truly repentant or not.

Bancroft outlines thirteen detailed steps an abuser must take in accepting responsibility for his actions that will lead to lasting change, including a full

[36] Lundy Bancroft, *Why Does He Do That? Inside the Minds of Angry and Controlling Men* (New York: G. P. Putnam's Sons, 2002), 334.

admission of the abuse and that it was wrong – unconditionally. The abuser must then acknowledge that his behavior was a choice, not a loss of control and recognize the effects it had on his victim(s). Developing respectful behaviors in their place seems to mirror the Bible's teaching of "putting off" sinful behaviors and "putting on" God-honoring ones (Ephesians 4:22), but rarely does the local church seem to take domestic abuse seriously to the extent secular programs do. Bancroft, like other abuse counselors in the field, concede that while lasting change is possible, overcoming abusiveness is often a life-long process and generally only occurs when the risk of the wife leaving is real.

Of course, we as Christians would cite the motivation for overcoming sin (of any stripe) as being a desire to glorify God. We would agree that in order to honor God, we must put aside any heart-attitudes and behaviors that clearly go against His Word. Few Christian men, no matter how volatile, would argue that beating one's wife is objectively sinful. However, tormenting others through unedifying speech such as sarcasm; covert aggression; rages (which they see as "righteous anger"); threats; intimidation; humiliation; false accusations – all of this can be rationalized away in their minds, because their victims somehow "deserve" it. Do they want to obey God? In many cases, yes. The thinking of the abusive Christian man is often so convoluted that he simply does not see his verbal torment as 'abuse'. Therefore, he sees no need to change.

How Nouthetic Counseling Can Add to the Problem

Churches that subscribe to a nouthetic counseling model often do far more harm than good to abuse survivors. Nouthetic counseling takes the view that all problems are ultimately sin problems. The way in which we are taught to "counsel" is essentially to answer each problem with Scriptures. While naturally we are to admonish one another to live according to God's Word, the problem with this approach is that it does not take into account the depth of some problems and perpetrators' unwillingness to change. It does not address the sensitive nuances of painful realities such as depression, and completely disregards feelings and emotions.

One woman, also trained as a nouthetic counselor and also trapped in an abusive marriage, anonymously wrote about the way she was "counseled":

> They told me, 'we cannot change anyone else; we can only change ourselves.' So . . . if, say, my husband were abusing me . . . . . MY job was to work only on my reaction and make sure it is not sinful... they always managed to get me to focus on my own

'sin issues'. For example, when I told them about my husband's pornography problems, they suggested that I wasn't available enough to my husband.

Victim-Shaming

This is exactly the sort of response I received at my former church. Although my ex-husband wasn't using pornography, the principle was the same: in multiple emails after I had detailed both my ex's ongoing intimidation attempts, bad-mouthing and slander of me, the pastor chided *me* for my "sinful response." When I stood up to the pastor for harassing and bullying me, I was told I had a "desperate heart" and was a "sheep who had wandered from the fold." This "blame-the-victim" routine is, sadly, par for the course at many churches that endorse nouthetic counseling (often termed "biblical counseling," although aspects of it seem anything but Christ-honoring). Because of this twisting of what it means to live the Christian life, abuse victims are often re-victimized by their churches' stance that it is good to sacrifice in order to feed another individual's narcissistic tendencies.

After I told my two pastors (one being a certified ACBC counselor) about the verbal and emotional abuse I had endured, the teaching pastor tried to admonish me in a private meeting with just the two of them: "You're a biblical counselor! Just because [ex-husband] has said, repeatedly, that he will not change, does not mean that God cannot change him! Would you tell the wife of an alcoholic, wife-beating man that he is hopeless, and would never change?"

My answer now, as then, is that I would actually have *more* hope for the wife-beating drunkard than for the sanctimonious, controlling man who destroys his wife and children through verbal abuse and stone-walling. Why? Because the first man knows he has a problem. For the same reason Jesus said the prostitutes and tax collectors were more likely to enter heaven than the Pharisees, such a man is more likely to concede that he is a miserable wretch of a husband, and seek to change himself than the more insidious abuser who hides in plain sight in the pews of a church. The latter sees himself as a pillar of integrity; a fine upstanding Christian and member of society. He sees his verbal and emotional abuse as necessary, and congratulates himself on how well he 'disciplines' his wife and children and is the 'spiritual leader' of his household. He may not even realize the depth of his sin, so great is his deception.

Even as a certified counselor myself, and one who has studied the Bible and taught courses on hermeneutics, I was forced to take part in nouthetic counseling myself in the months following my divorce. Wanting to stay at my former church, (and having been told if I was patient enough and went along with the process, sooner or later my abuser's unrepentance would vindicate me), I naively agreed. The pastor made it clear that the goal of counseling was *not* for my personal healing from the abuse; but rather, to address my "sinful reactions" to the abuse. The counselor even indicated that by my leaving, I was partially at fault for my ex-husband's accelerated verbal abuse towards our college-aged daughter (an implication that horrified both my pastor and two other biblical counselors). There really is very little uniformity of thought in the "nouthetic" stream of counseling.

Finding Godly Help in the Church

This is not to say, of course, that no evangelical churches help abuse victims or offer helpful counsel. Fortunately, there are very good counseling ministries in which victims of abusive marriages can find truly godly help, and are able to put the past behind them and heal (we will discuss the healing process in a later chapter). Charis Counseling (*charis* meaning *grace* in Greek) is one such ministry, with state-licensed mental health professionals who are active, professing believers in Christ and adhere to a conservative, Protestant Statement of Faith. The American Association of Christian Counselors has a vast number of well-trained, compassionate counselors in most states, and even Christian support groups for women fleeing abusive marriages (many of whom have experienced secondary spiritual abuse from their churches) have sprung up. One such group in the Boston area, Hagar's Sisters, offers one-on-one counsel as well as group meetings free of charge. Cleansing Stream Ministries offers seminars and programs online dedicated to helping abuse survivors heal. The Christian support group DivorceCare ministers to believers who have gone through a divorce, and addresses the sensitive issue of healing from abuse very biblically. And para-church ministries such as Give Her Wings provide practical help to women who have had to escape abuse as well as spiritual support and counsel.

Moreover, the tide is beginning to change within influential Christian ministries. During the writing of this book, the Australian arm of The Gospel Coalition published "An Open Letter to Husbands Who Abuse Their Wives," which originated with the (American) Association of Biblical Counselors (ABC).[37] It is encouraging to see a major, conservative Christian ministry call abusive men to account who remain members in good standing of their respective churches. The author of the piece stated clearly from the

---

[37] https://australia.thegospelcoalition.org/article/a-letter-to-husbands-who-abuse-their-wives

outset that God is against any man who uses biblical passages to control, abuse and manipulate his wife. We need more hard-hitting, realistic writing like this within evangelicalism.

Perhaps because the problem of clergy and lay-man abuse within the Church has received so much attention in Australia in recent years, more Australian pastors and influential church leaders are speaking and writing publically about the problem. Dr. Graham Hill Ph.D., who is the provost of Morling College in Sydney Australia and the founding director of The Global Church Project, recently published a moving apology to victims of domestic violence within the Church – freely acknowledging the local churches' failure to act appropriately. "I'm sorry and sad that we Christian leaders have sometimes behaved in ways that have made your suffering and shame worse," he wrote. "I'm sorry for the way we've often failed to listen to your experiences as women." He was not alone. In one Campbelltown parish, Reverend Nigel Fortescue (who had regularly seen women in his congregation victimized by domestic violence) issued a call to action: "Dear Friends, some Christians are aggressive and violent towards their family. Fact...It's unacceptable. It's ungodly. It's horrific. It's got to stop. Our response to domestic violence among church members and the erroneous teaching of some pastors cannot only be institutional, committee-led, inquiry-based and happening later. Our response must happen now."

Closer to home, the Association of Baptist Churches in the United States has organized campaigns to end domestic violence, and issued their own Domestic Violence Guide for Churches to train pastors and counselors to spot warning signs and effectively counsel victims and perpetrators of all manners of domestic abuse (see chapter 10 for more information).

The Facade is Believable

Unfortunately, the experience of all too many within the visible Church is different – the ongoing problem of verbal, mental and even physical abuse is routinely minimized or swept under the rug. Jeff Crippin has decades of pastoral experience, and has written books and sermon series on the problem of abuse in the church. He cites several reasons as to why local churches are often havens for abusive men:

> As domestic abuse victims know all too well, churches are one of the most abuser-friendly environments. Even when they are reported multiple times, they are most often not prosecuted and the victim is disbelieved. When they do go to prison, they frequently return to a church that does not know them once they

are out of prison, and begin the cycle all over again. Churches usually don't bother to check the person's criminal history because the nice, "Christian" facade is so well played.

...a number of reasons why Christians are so gullible:

1. The abuser's double life. "Niceness and likability will override a track record of molestation/abuse any day of the week."

2. Children usually do not report being molested, especially when the perpetrator holds a position of trust in the church.

3. Molesters realize that "church people" are easier to fool than most other people because they have a trusting mentality. They want to believe in the "good that exists in all people." [Something the Bible certainly does NOT teach, by the way!]

4. Despite the fact that decades of research have demonstrated that people cannot reliably tell who is lying and who isn't, most people believe they can.

All of these factors also come into play in the case of domestic abusers who pose as Christians. Almost every Christian who has been victimized by an abuser will testify to this wall of refusal to believe such evil could be happening, let alone perpetrated by "such a fine Christian." [38]

The Abuser as False Convert

This pattern also calls into question how many professing Christians who are either abusive or enabling/covering up abuse in their midst actually have a relationship with Christ. Their fruit seems to indicate they are deceiving themselves, even twisting Scripture to justify oppression of those weaker (whether women or children) with legalism and man-made dogma. However, the Bible is clear on the spiritual condition of the abuser and his allies: "Whoever makes a practice of sinning is of the devil, for the devil has been sinning from the beginning. The reason the Son of God appeared was to destroy the works of the devil. No one born of God makes a practice of sinning, for God's seed abides in him, and he cannot keep on sinning because he has been born of God." (1 John 3:8-9)

[38] https://cryingoutforjustice.com/2012/05/24/why-churches-are-abuser-friendly-environments-by-jeff-crippen/

As stated earlier, there is, of course, great hope for an abuser (of either sex) to turn from his or her cruel ways and experience lasting change. Yet when one is so deceived about one's own behavior that they do not see it clearly as sin, as God does, there is no impetus to change. Furthermore, while some degree of temporary behavior modification may be possible for an unregenerate person, apart from the work of the Holy Spirit (through a saving relationship with Jesus Christ), the abuser's heart will not change towards his or her spouse.

This is what makes the superficial view of repentance many churches seem to have so dangerous – the assumption that a church-going abuser is actually saved (and has actually experienced regeneration and heart change by saying "I'm sorry") glosses over the serious nature of his or her condition. Most abusive men in the church are highly-skilled at speaking "Christianeze" lingo, and even quoting Scripture. They frequently have two different countenances: their "Sunday face," by which they are known to be affable, pleasant family men; and the brooding, bitter persona that comes out at home behind closed doors. Control, manipulation and enforcing power over another individual (whether physically, psychologically, or both) is a deep-seated, life-dominating sin that needs intense counseling and a true desire for change to overcome. A few weeks (or months) of pastoral counseling, no matter how well-intentioned, will not undo a worldview and behavior pattern that has yielded great rewards for the abuser. As mentioned earlier, many (if not most) abusers have been characterized as having some degree of narcissistic tendencies. The narcissistic personality type is notoriously difficult to change, as both Christian and secular counselors will attest.

The Distortion of Matthew 18

One of the strangest misapplications of Scripture that has emerged in primarily American Reformed evangelical churches is using verses from the gospel of Matthew to "exhort," or intimidate, abused wives into going back to their husbands. While they pay lip-service to the necessity of repentance on the abuser's part, in reality the "reconciliation process" is a foregone conclusion to which the woman is expected to adhere. If she balks (as I did), she will be excommunicated. This is called "church discipline," and rather than being applied to the one who is truly in sin (the abusive partner), it is commonly applied to the victim.

This growing phenomenon seems to be more prevalent in what some Christian bloggers have termed "Neo-Calvinist" churches. Again, I try to avoid the label only because it adds confusion and has little to do with the historic Calvinism of Geneva. In the United States, a growing trend among the so-called "young, restless and Reformed" is to implement a system of church discipline which in many cases is a misinterpretation of Matthew 18:15-20.

Molly Worthen, an assistant professor of American religious history at the University of North Carolina at Chapel Hill and author of *Apostles of Reason: The Crisis of Authority in American Evangelicalism* spoke to the media covering my story about this recent trend. However, Worthen clarified the difference between Reformed theology *per se* and the term "Neo-Calvinist." "[Neo-Calvinist] tends to refer not to the historic ethnically Dutch (Calvinist) church," she explained. "It tends to refer more to conservative evangelicals, often southern Baptists who have chosen this as a way to support certain theological and social points. There's a lot of pressure for women just to accept things and accept the authority of men." Worthen also said these churches tend to settle personal matters (such as marriage or abuse counseling) inside the congregation, rather than reaching outside the church for help.

The distortion of these five verses from Matthew's gospel, about personal conflict resolution among Christians, has caused untold pain and humiliation to many innocent people (including abused women) in churches that subscribe to it. In their theological construct, suffering is redemptive. Submission to one's husband is an absolute. If you stand up to the suffering inflicted by your husband, you must be the one in sin – and therefore, subject to castigation. Object to being cast as the villain, and it is only used as further evidence of the "desperate situation of your heart."

"Gaslighting," as we saw in chapter 2, is a term used by psychologists and therapists to describe the subtle (and sometimes overt) methods of psychological intimidation abusers use to make their victims question their own sanity. Authoritative clergy are especially skilled in this, because inflicting guilt and the fear of divine punishment is a control mechanism to keep the 'sheep' in line. If an institution claiming to act in the Name of Christ is systematically tormenting the weakest and most vulnerable members of His Body, the sheep will be so beaten down that eventually they will leave.

Crippin describes the pattern that all too often befalls women in churches that take a rigid stance on church discipline (especially in cases of separation/ divorce for reasons of abuse):

What a Victim Can Expect in a Typical Evangelical Church

Let me list for you the typical cycle of what an abuse victim can expect when she reports the abuse to her church (pastor, elders), seeking help and justice. Those knowledgeable about abuse know that there is a "cycle of abuse" effected at the hands of the victim's church. Here is the drama that I have had victim after victim recount to me:

1. Victim reports abuse to her pastor.

2. Pastor does not believe her claims, or at least believes that they are greatly exaggerated. After all, he "knows" her husband to be one of the finest Christian men he knows, a pillar of the church.

3. Pastor minimizes the severity of the abuse. His goal is often, frankly, damage control (to himself and his church).

4. Pastor indirectly (or not so indirectly!) implies that the victim needs to do better in her role as wife and mother and as a Christian. He concludes that all such scenarios are a "50/50" blame sharing.

5. Pastor sends the victim home, back to the abuser, after praying with her and entrusting the problem to the Lord.

6. Pastor believes he has done his job.

7. Victim returns, reporting that nothing has changed. She has tried harder and prayed, but the abuse has continued.

8. Pastor decides to do some counseling. He says "I will have a little talk with your husband" or "I am sure that the three of us can sit down and work this all out." Either of these routes only results in further and more intense abuse of the victim. This counseling can go on for years! (One victim reported that it dragged on for nine years in her case.)

9. As time passes, the victim becomes the guilty party in the eyes of the pastor and others. She is the one causing the commotion. She is pressured by the pastor and others in the church to stop rebelling, to submit to her husband, and stop causing division in the church.

10. After more time passes, the victim separates from or divorces the abuser. The church has refused to believe

her, has persistently covered up the abuse, has failed to obey the law and report the abuse to the police, and has refused to exercise church discipline against the abuser. Ironically, warnings of impending church discipline are often directed against the victim!

11. The final terrible injustice is that the victim is the one who must leave the church, while the abuser remains a member in good standing, having successfully duped the pastor and church into believing that his victim was the real problem. One abuse victim (a man in this case) told me that he finally came to the awakening that "I know exactly what my church is going to do about my abuser: Nothing!" He left while she remained a member in good standing, the daughter of a leading pastor in the denomination.

I observed a similar pattern firsthand following an incident of abuse. Over time, concern for the victim diminishes and *the primary focus turns to the plight of the perpetrator, the consequences he must suffer now, and how we can help him.* At the same time, *the victim is increasingly pushed aside and even accused of causing all this unpleasantness.* In Christian settings, the victim is accused of being unforgiving and of refusing to obey Scripture's commands to reconcile. The victim becomes a leper and often is ultimately driven outside the camp. It is horrible injustice. What must Christ think of it? [39] (Emphasis mine).

When I first read Crippin's abridged account of what he, in his lengthy ministry, has observed to be many churches' response to marital abuse, I had a very visceral reaction. He had described my personal experience in a suburban, "Neo-Calvinist" church in Massachusetts so perfectly I could have written the narrative myself. What I didn't know, as I admitted earlier in this chapter, was just how common this practice and distortion of Matthew 18's teaching really is. Many emails and contact with other women who have been through similar experiences have confirmed just how commonly this form of Scripture-coated victim-blaming occurs.

The goal of Matthew 18 is *restoration*, not a threat of public humiliation. When reading the passage, the *de facto* nature of its intent seems wholly out of context with attempting to resolve marital difficulties by sending

<hr />

[39] Jeff Crippin, *A Cry for Justice: How the Evil of Domestic Abuse Hides in Your Church* (Greenville: Calvary Press, 2012), 21-22.

the victimized women back to her abuser. Claiming that God has "called us to pursue you," (as some pastors do in threatening letters to abused women after they resign their church membership), is wholly unsupported in Scripture and has nothing to do with love or restoration. Going to one's brother and attempting to resolve interpersonal conflict seems a logical first step between man and wife when conflicts first arise (even allowing for an imbalance of power). When the abuser fails to listen or simply justifies his behavior, then it seems appropriate for church leadership to step in (and separation between the husband and wife to occur, in many circumstances).

A No-Win Situation

The reader may rest assured that every wife who has experienced *any* kind of abuse, whether mental or physical, has already done due diligence in attempting such conflict resolution. When change is not forthcoming, she may bring in the witness of "one or two" others. Now we see how this passage, while certainly applicable to objective matters of dispute, cannot possibly apply to marital abuse. Who witnesses it? With the possible exception of the children (who should never be called in as "witnesses" against a parent), *usually no one*. What friends witness is often relegated to "gut feelings," observations, or "vibes," if the abuse is not physical. How can one be called in as a witness to behavior that usually takes place (by design) behind closed doors?

Once it is "told to the church" (or confided in the pastor or elders), life may become an Orwellian existence for the woman who expected help and protection. Since they cannot, in any real sense, monitor her husband's abusive tendencies towards her, they can only take him at his word when he shows up in the counseling office with a hangdog look and purports to want to "do anything it takes to save my family." One nouthetic counselor writing about my personal situation, said:

> Their "job" (and ours as biblical counselors) is to preserve marriages and push for restoration and reconciliation whenever possible. The fact that [name redacted] is saying he doesn't want the divorce also slants things in his favor with the church. You and I can understand that is what abusers do, and why, but your church has little to no experience with this and has no idea. They see a man whose wife left him and is claiming abuse. That same man now sits in front of them telling them he wants to save his marriage. He says he wants marriage counseling. You telling

them there is no way you will consider that does not go well for you with them.

This was from a female counselor who herself had been divorced from an abuser and had since re-married. She specialized in counseling emotionally abused women. Her observations proved eerily true, although I tried to give the benefit of the doubt to my former pastors and the man they claimed to be counseling.

"9 Marks" and Its Influence

About a year after my divorce was finalized, I noticed my ex-husband had started posting links from a ministry called 9 Marks on social media. 9 Marks has a cult-following in the wake of the book *9 Marks of a Healthy Church* by "Neo-Cal" pastor Mark Dever. While on the surface many of their teachings seem to be scripturally sound, they take biblical principles and skew them to an extreme that Christ never endorsed nor intended. Church discipline and an unhealthy emphasis on "church covenants" (which are never mentioned in the Bible) are part of their primary doctrine of what makes a church "healthy."

My former husband had never taken an interest in theology before; certainly not Protestant blogs or Reformed ministry writings. He had never heard of 9 Marks (or "9 Marx", as it is known by its critics). Knowing that my former pastor was a proponent of 9 Marks, I could easily see the grooming pattern. As Jesus chided the Pharisees, "Woe to you, scribes and Pharisees, hypocrites! For you travel across sea and land to make a single proselyte, and when he becomes a proselyte, you make him twice as much a child of hell as yourselves." (Matthew 23:15).

The tragedy of such a situation is that if true men of the Gospel had intervened a decade earlier, and shared the reality of Christ's unwavering love with my then-husband, perhaps he, like many in his predicament, could have been saved from the bondage of man-made traditions that will only affirm his abusive tendencies. The high-control religious group he is currently in will only feed him more of the same, and as a man who prizes control above all other idols, he will continue to absorb this type of material and tell himself that it represents the Gospel.

There is hope. Now, in the days of mass communication and especially given the ease of access to survivors' testimonies via the Internet, more light is being shed onto the insidious way domestic abuse goes undetected (or is denied) in Christian churches. Increasingly, more survivors of both spousal abuse and the subsequent pain of secondary abuse by the church leaders they trusted are coming forward and speaking out.

CHAPTER 7

"Denial" is Not Just a River in Egypt – How Abusers Minimize their Behavior

"Maybe I made some mistakes, but it wasn't 'abuse.'
She takes everything too seriously! I told the pastor that was
just a joke, and we laughed about it. Besides, she wasn't
submissive enough to me! She deserved all that and more."
– An abusive ex-husband in denial

As any counselor who has worked with men who abuse women will testify, one of the most difficult parts of counseling is getting the abuser to see that *he* is the problem – not his victim. He has believed his own hype for so long that he actually believes that his reviling speech and contemptuous treatment of his partner is somehow justified.

We have already seen that the abuser's motivating factor is *control*. The justification that enables him to pursue control over another is his sense of *entitlement*. Through years of repeated behavior and lying to himself ("I'm a good husband/provider/lover...if I yell a little and put her in her place, that's not really abuse – that's what I have to do,") he has reinforced the layers of self-deception under which he operates. He actually believes, especially if the abuse is non-physical that his behavior is justified – and is not really abusive. Such individuals will always blame their behavior on others, while insisting it was not really wrong.

Although some batterers do claim that beating their wives or girlfriends is not abuse ("She had it coming to her!"), the obvious physical evidence, laws against domestic violence and constraints of decent society prohibit him from convincing others that beating a woman is not "really abuse." Unfortunately, the same cannot be said of the scars caused by continual verbal and psychological abuse, where outsiders are not as readily able to see the devious ways tormentors will try and minimize or excuse their sin.

Manipulators of the Truth

Psychologically abusive and manipulative men are usually extremely intelligent, especially those with narcissistic tendencies. They are experts at twisting the truth; casting their victims in the role of villain, and gaining allies to their sides. Other than children, who can easily be manipulated by the more "powerful" parent in a marriage with a significant imbalance of power (which abusive marriages always are), there are not many eye-witnesses to the worst of the torment. As we have already seen, emotionally abusive men have multiple faces – the one their wives see behind closed doors; and the one the church congregation and their co-workers see in public. Sometimes, the façade will slip just enough for neighbors to see (or suspect) the truth about the abuser's true character, but for the most part, it remains hidden. Therefore, when their victims stand up and speak out about the way they are being treated, it is relatively easy for them to twist the story enough to put themselves in the role of "poor suffering martyr" and their wives as the rebellious ones who have chosen the wrong path. As hundreds upon hundreds of women in Christian churches have attested, they find themselves in a no-win situation: the abuser is often now being enabled by the very church from which she sought help.

Sinful Abuse, or Unfortunate "Mistake"?

Carefully crafting his words, the abuser before his spiritual leaders will readily admit to having "made mistakes" in his marriage and even with his children. He will even confess to "sin" in a general sense. He will often admit to getting angry too easily, but is quick to find a justification for his anger – she didn't have dinner prepared on time; the kids' grades were slipping; she spent too much time on social media. He will see no connection between his heart issue (selfish desire to be the center of attention and in control of everyone, to the point of micro-management) and how out of proportion his anger was to the situation. And yet, such concessions will often be readily accepted by pastors as "evidence of repentance." They are not. The abuser knows exactly what he is doing.

Leveling hateful, false accusations against his wife and children will not be labeled "abuse"; it will again be put into the category of "mistake." This allows him to avoid full responsibility for the seriousness of his sin – a *mistake* is unintentional. Verbal abuse is *very* intentional. His words are sharply-wielded swords; chosen deliberately to cause the most pain. With every tongue-lashing he knows exactly how to draw the most blood. He has studied his victim and knows her weaknesses and vulnerabilities perfectly; he has planned ahead of time how he will amplify them the next time he berates her (while down-playing his own faults, of course). He will take full advantage of his ability to hurt her to the core by bringing up every past indiscretion and personal failing, so that she will be left an emotional cripple weeping in the corner. (My ex-husband, to give a less-extreme example, delighted in reminding me of youthful mistakes I had made 20 years earlier, and would lash out at me for hours if I forgot some household responsibility such as paying a bill. It was supposedly evidence I "didn't care about the family".)

Keeping Up Appearances

Since the abuser must retain power at all costs, he must never allow his true self to be seen by outsiders. Therefore, when beginning the "counseling/ reconciliation" process that is the standard response in conservative evangelical churches, he will play the game very skillfully from the very beginning. His goal is singular: to get his victim back. Abusers never want their victims to leave; in doing so, they not only lose the object of their control and power – they stand to lose face within the Christian community. They must never allow this to happen. The church must always see them as the protagonist; their victim as the antagonist. This starts with the abuser controlling the narrative.

The abusive husband will often go to the pastor, hat in hand, professing willingness to do whatever is necessary to get his wife back. He will most heartily agree to counseling; as surely there is some "communication issue" they must work through. (This is common, even if the couple has been in years of Christian marriage counseling, and he has never stopped his abuse.) He will re-double his efforts to paint himself as a model husband and father, while casting his victim in the most unfavorable light possible.

If she has even once stood up to his hateful speech and treatment of her, she will surely be called "unsubmissive" or even "rebellious." The abuser has often been a church-goer for years, and thus knows exactly what terminology to use and which buttons to push when speaking to a patriarchal authoritarian church leader. The pastor will quite readily conclude that this earnest, contrite man sitting before him could not possibly have destroyed his marriage – certainly not by the kind of ongoing, escalating abuse his wife describes – and concludes that there must be "bi-lateral sin"[40] in the situation.

Rather than seeing that he is dealing with a "reviler," a "rager" and/or a "contentious man" who hates his wife, the pastor then concludes that the wife must be partly at fault. Very few pastors have any form of abuse training in seminary, and while some have studied nouthetic counseling they often graduate from seminary with pat answers they are certain will "work" in any situation. Therefore, since the maxim "God hates divorce" has been drilled into them to the exclusion of the Bible's teaching about unrighteous anger, they will set about to salvage the marriage at all costs – which means, for them, finding a way to justify sending the victim back to her abuser. Gullible enough to believe the abuser is just a garden-variety "sinner" who is surely repentant, they then begin the pursuit of the victim – while both abuser and victim know that no real change has, or ever will, occur in this deeply disturbed man.

These men will then continue to abuse, lashing out at their victims – although ever more smugly now, knowing that they are gaining the support of the spiritual leaders (who may even be questioning the validity of their wives' testimony by this point). Powerless to change anything, the woman is rendered voiceless – at the mercy of those "leaders" who will stand judge and jury (without knowing anything about the psychology of abusive men, or why they do what they do). The abuser is thus enabled and emboldened by the church leaders, and will find ever new ways to torment his wife (or ex-wife).

Reactive Abuse

As I touched on in the last chapter, a very common aspect of psychological abuse and manipulation is for the abuser to claim that the victim is being abusive towards them. This is a key strategy in minimizing his own sin. As absurd as it sounds, calling their victim "abusive" for snapping or reacting to their continual abuse is a common gaslighting tactic called *reactive abuse*. A woman married to a controlling man who constantly demeans and nit-picks her will typically endure and endure, but the moment she snaps back at him or stands up for herself she will be told she is over-reacting and, in fact, is abusing *him*. The abusive man's innate sense of entitlement and

---

[40]   A word invented to imply that some sin on the part of the woman, real or imagined, is at least partially for her husband's diabolical treatment of her. It is a form of victim-blaming that allows pastors/nouthetic counselors to avoid the unpleasant reality that abusers abuse because it is their nature; not the fault of their victims. There is nothing a wife could do that would biblically justify true verbal and emotional abuse.

self-righteousness enables him to mentally reverse his own aggression and project it onto his victim.

After years of humiliation and constant put-downs, many women's self-worth is so completely destroyed that she will actually believe she is sinning or being the aggressor for protecting herself. An abusive man will jump on any reaction from his victim in self-defense, and use it to prove she is unstable. Also, their targets are not always weak, cowering women: many abusive and power-seeking men treat women who are strong-willed and psychologically hard to manipulate as a special challenge. It is a common misconception that abusers primarily prey on the vulnerable. They often see women with successful careers who are well-respected and popular among peers as a threat to them, so they will set out to "break" them.

Shannon Thomas, therapist and author of *Healing from Hidden Abuse*, writes that success and strength are actually what attract abusive narcissists and psychopaths to their targets. Victims of psychological abuse are often strong, confident and successful, and tend to be empathetic. According to Thomas, an abuser would want to drag out negative traits in someone (and accuse them of reactive abuse) because to them a relationship is all about feeling superior. People who engage in psychological abuse of their partners, colleagues, friends, or family, are often narcissistic and believe everyone is beneath them.[41]

Even in cases of physical abuse, when victims attempt to thwart (sometimes life-threatening) attacks, the abuser will define her actions as violence towards *him*. This is more common, however, in cases of non-physical abuse. Of course he "had to" slam the door or yell at his kids. He was provoked, at least through the lens with which he views others. Why would the abuser think that the victim is now the "abuser", if he is conscience-stricken about his reviling and unwholesome speech against her? Because in his mind, she is inferior – she was the one supposed to be listening mutely; accepting without question whatever venom he spews at her. She "deserved" it. After all, she was the one who hadn't vacuumed the floor after getting home from work. If she tells him that his treatment of her is unwarranted and sinful, now she is the one abusing him. With just enough of a spin on the facts, he can easily get the pastor to believe his perception of reality.

"It Was All a Joke"

When held accountable, another way abusers minimize their behavior (and mask their motives) is by claiming the often-irrational things they said in

---

[41] http://www.businessinsider.com/strong-confident-people-end-up-in-abusive-relationships-2017-8?r=UK&IR=T

anger were "joking." This is surprisingly common, even when the context and testimony indicates their tantrum was anything but a joke. This alibi has a double-benefit to the abuser – not only can he portray himself to the counselor as a misunderstood chap with a sense of humor, his victim may now be seen as overly-sensitive or emotional. This is rarely, if ever, the case. Any woman who has had to endure years of verbal abuse from a husband (or father) has built up a very thick skin, and it takes tremendous courage for her to finally start standing up to the tirades. One abuser I know personally knew full well he was lying to the pastor when he told him his tirade against his daughter was "a joke" – the sneering, evil look of triumph on his face when he relayed how he even got the pastor to laugh (at his poor daughter's expense) told me he took pleasure in his own calculated duplicity.

Failure to See Himself as Source of Conflict

Abusive men love to label their wives as "contentious," as somehow being the party responsible in situations where there is conflict. Good counselors attempt to analyze abusers' responses to conflict, and try to get them to handle disagreements differently. They need to be able to identify where God is in the situation; if they are handling their sinful emotions in a Christ-honoring way; and how to respond in a godly manner to their spouses. But because of the way an abuser's mind is programmed, this is a very difficult task for them to do. While they remain in denial that they are at fault (or even guilty of full-fledged abuse), it remains impossible.

Abusers use an array of conversational control tactics, such as denying being angry at all – and then find something else about their wives to criticize. They insult and belittle their wives (or patronize them, telling them that they'd be "nothing" without their help and "support"), and accuse them of being helpless or immature. The final card-trick is, of course, accusing their victims of reactive abuse when they become angry or defend themselves. If she has been conditioned for years to unquestioningly view her husband as the strong, stable and "correct" one, the woman will struggle greatly under the weight of this torture before seeing it for what it really is – and standing up for herself. This is especially true if the woman has never seen a godly marriage patterned in her own life. If a woman grew up in a home devoid of mutual respect and godly communication between her parents, she is unlikely to realize how toxic verbal torment is to her spirit until it is too late. She will likely blame herself, even though she knows deep down her husband is initiating conflict just to smash her down and show her (sometimes in front of his friends and family) "who's the boss."

The Effect on Children

Exposure to psychological abuse between parents is more damaging to children's wellbeing as they grow older than physical domestic violence, according to new research carried out at the University of Limerick in Ireland. The study indicated that psychological abuse can include name-calling, intimidation, isolation, manipulation and control. According to a scientific paper published by The Journal of Interpersonal Violence on the findings of the study, children who grow up in homes where emotional/psychological abuse occurs have more extensive long-term consequences than those who grow up witnessing physical violence.

> Our research found that young people (aged 17 to 25 years) reported experiencing two distinct yet interrelated types of domestic abuse in their families of origin: physical which includes hitting, punching, kicking and use of a weapon; and, psychological abuse including arguing, name-calling or behaviour that is intimidating, isolating, manipulating or controlling. Importantly, our findings show that it was young people's exposure to the psychological dimension of domestic abuse, which had a detrimental impact on their psychological wellbeing. Exposure to the physical dimension did not have any additional negative effect on wellbeing.[42]

This is surprising, as it seems counter-intuitive: wouldn't witnessing Dad hitting Mom on a regular basis affect children more strongly than verbal beat-downs? Apparently, no.

Although the effects of familial abuse may be long-term rather than short-term, it should be noted that children and teenagers have an amazing capacity for cognitive dissonance. They see what goes on and hear what is said, and instinctively know something is terribly wrong; yet wanting desperately to love both parents, they tend to minimize the reality of the abuse. One way this occurs is through terminology – using language to downplay the seriousness of abusive behavior.

Word Play

As Orwell, politicians and propaganda experts alike well know, words hold power. If one changes the words, or tweaks the meaning of a word with an

---

[42] "Exposure to Domestic Violence and Abuse: Evidence of Distinct Physical and Psychological Dimensions", Journal of Interpersonal Violence. Catherine M. Naughton, Aisling T. O'Donnell, Orla T. Muldoon. May 5, 2017.

established acceptable meaning, he or she can effectively manipulate the way hearers think and process information. For example, the seemingly-innocuous term "egalitarian" carries the implication that women are equal to men. Of course we are. But it has been adapted to mean that women may stand in final authority of the local church. Similarly, the term "feminist," as it is commonly used today, implies a bra-burning radical who stands for pro-abortion rights – far from its original meaning as a supporter of suffrage and equal job compensation and opportunities for women. Also, some words are "loaded" – assumed by society in general to already hold a certain connotation. Re-naming ugly realities causes a subtle disconnect in their target audience. For example, "abortion" may become "termination"; "murder of civilians" becomes "collateral damage"; "firing" becomes "made redundant."

In similar fashion, the abuser (and the church leaders who may enable him) downplay "verbal abuse" to "losing one's temper" or "yelling"; tyrannical control to "headship"; and even coercion to "misunderstanding." Flagrant abuse, in the eyes of a child, may become re-named "mistreatment" or simply "Dad going a little bit too far". This type of word selection serves to blunt the harsh reality that Dad abused Mom, whether he wants to admit it or not. Such semantics and "softening" of sin is all too easy to rationalize when the abuse was not physical, nor was it targeted (at least primarily) towards the children.

Unfortunately, the dominant spouse (usually the abusive one) generally holds more credence over the children, whether out of an automatic deference mentality or subliminal fear. This is especially true when the woman has separated from the abuser, and they either share joint custody or equal time with the children. I have heard from many women who testify that their former abusers have effectively been able to manipulate the children against them, without the children even being aware that they are being manipulated. One woman wrote, "He calls me names to the kids when they are with him, which they repeat. He fabricates stories about me; bad-mouths my friends, my family...even implies that I'm a bad mother. But the kids don't even realize what's going on, he's so clever!"

Ironically, children (including teenagers) seem adept at minimizing or justifying the abuser's faults or sins, while magnifying or even exaggerating the victim's (usually the mother). Remember, an abuser must always control the narrative in order to maintain his sense of "control." With his own children, who are pre-disposed to believe him as a near demi-god of sorts, this is often all too easy – especially when the abuser has successfully cajoled his church leaders to his cause. One Midwestern mother wrote me that her estranged husband even prevents the children from seeing their court-ordered therapist, so determined is he to convince them their mother "abandoned" him. Sadly, the children of emotionally-abused mothers often lack the maturity and critical thinking skills to understand the toxicity of the relationship their mother was in. Most church counseling ministries are woefully unequipped to deal with this reality.

In the next chapter, we will examine an all-too-typical scenario from my own experience that demonstrates how churches often mishandle cases of marital abuse.

CHAPTER 8

When a Church Mishandles Abuse: A Case Study

"A sociopath is defined by their lack of empathy. I marvel at the lack of empathy that allows a leader or person in a position of authority to give a tepid or indifferent response to someone reporting abuse. Worse, some of them actively support the batterer... when they know about the abuse and are in a position to step in, but won't. I believe that the cowardly are expressing the darkness in their own faithless heart and they are an accessory to a crime. It takes faith to expose and stand against abuse in a culture of silence."
– Anonymous survivor of domestic and clergy abuse

We have already seen how patriarchal and authoritarian attitudes and teachings have become broadly accepted in certain branches of Protestantism, and how wives of men with angry, controlling or downright abusive tendencies are conditioned to accept this treatment in the name of "suffering for the sake of righteousness" or "being a 1 Peter wife." While being careful to specify that not all (or even most) evangelical churches hold to these positions or tolerate abuse, the unfortunate truth is that many American churches do. Some have a particular propensity to pursue the woman (who is usually the victim) for "repentance" when she finds the courage to report or leave her abuser. As pointed out earlier, it is most frequently the woman who is singled out and vilified after already enduring domestic abuse. This is done through a systematic process called "church discipline" based on a misapplication of Matthew 18:15-20 (see chapter 6).

Reconciliation or Excommunication

My own experience in an abusive marriage (and subsequently being bullied out of a church) typifies what all too many women go through in churches that take the "no divorce for abuse" stance. The real issue in these cases, as we will see, is less whether abuse *per se* constitutes "biblical grounds for divorce" than it is whether the abuser is truly repentant. While paying lip-service to reconciliation being conditional upon repentance, my experience, like that of so many others, is that *reconciliation under any circumstances* is seen as a foregone conclusion by some authoritarian pastors. The abuse may be ongoing, yet the victim is expected to report on "what fruit and growth" she has seen in her abuser's life in order to play along.

The ongoing extent and details of the abuse, no matter how well-documented, are often considered completely irrelevant by church leaders. A woman in this position, no matter what she proves in her own defense or how well she knows the Scriptures, has no recourse. Eugene Peterson writes, "Religion is a very scary thing, because a pastor is in a position of power. And if you use that power badly, you ruin people's lives, and you ruin your own life." Unqualified leadership in a local church can, indeed, destroy lives and create immense fallout for *all* members – not just the abuse victims themselves.

Churches will often go to the extent of harassment or threats of defamation (illegal when a former member has already resigned) in order to reign the victim back into the unhealthy situation. Of course, the leadership of such authoritarian groups roundly deny this by pointing to the fact that they "allow for a temporary separation" whilst both parties are "counseled separately." In an Orwellian-style game of semantics, the woman is left with two choices: acquiesce to their demands for "reconciliation" and pretend the abuser has repented; or resign church membership (obtaining legal representation if the harassment continues) and start her life over again. These churches desperately need to learn Christ-like compassion for the oppressed and beaten-down women in their flocks.

My Experience

I spent 20 years in an emotionally and verbally abusive marriage, the details of which I re-capped in a 5,000 word statement for my former pastors when pressed. I lived on edge, with knots of fear in my stomach every single day, and it was only after months of separation that I finally felt the chronic anxiety subside.

Although he never hit or beat me, my former husband became increasingly angry and unstable during the two decades we were married. In 2008 I pleaded with him to go to biblical counseling at our church with me, and he sneered that "[I was] the crazy one who needed counseling." (I had been asking that we get some form of marriage counseling since 2002, when his anger problem started to get really serious, and was always told that I, not he, was the one who had the problem.)

For our four children's sake, I have decided not to disclose exhaustive details about what I endured when married to their father. Nevertheless, I noticed a definite increase both in the tyrannical pattern itself and in my ex-husband's attitude about his behavior during the ten years we spent in an authoritarian evangelical church. He seemed to find spiritual justification for his demeaning treatment of me in the patriarchal worldview held by the church, although the Bible studies he attended and sermons preached certainly weren't to blame themselves. Many men, who do not have controlling personalities, can apply the "headship" principles taught in such churches and still manage to have loving and mutually-fulfilling marriages. However, what I dealt with during that time was what one hospital chaplain called "the worst case of psychological abuse I have ever heard of in a Christian marriage, in over 25 years."

Many co-workers of mine, two women from the neighborhood and five women from the church, recognized and approached me over the years about the abuse. Several more came forward after the fact, saying they had had suspicions. After a failed nouthetic counseling attempt, I told my then-husband that I couldn't take it anymore; and, inasmuch as he had no intention of loving me as a wife and equal, we were divorcing. He agreed to a mediated divorce, in which I gave up almost all of the assets I was entitled to, and on February 1, 2016 I left with my car and personal belongings.

A month later, I went to my two pastors and told them why I had filed for divorce. I explained that we had already done months of counseling in 2014 and that my ex-husband had made it clear many times since that he was *not* going to change; nor did he see any issues with his behavior. The two pastors (one a teaching pastor and the other a counseling pastor) were surprised, but initially seemed understanding and compassionate. Eight days later, on March 16, 2016, I received an email from the counseling pastor, speaking on both his and the teaching pastor's behalf, asking me to come in for another meeting with just the two of them and "answer a few questions" to ensure that "this very final decision was made in a way that honors God and His Word."

I happened to be at work when I received this message, in the Interpreter Services office with my scheduling coordinator, Stephanie. One of my few colleagues to know about my divorce (and that I attended a conservative evangelical church), Stephanie, who has a Master's Degree in theology, advised me against attending the meeting. I laughed at her concerns, saying, "Listen, girl, I have almost the same training they do – I'm a certified nouthetic counselor. I know where they're going with this. Don't worry; they were nice to me last week. They *get* it! This was a clear-cut case of abuse; and they know my situation. I'll tell them anything they want to know."

Having spent a fair bit of time immersed in the conservative evangelical subculture, Stephanie was worried. "No, Marie. Why do you think they want to 'meet with you' two on one? This is not going to go well..... Marie, you have to get out of that church. You're not going to win this one." I remained unconcerned, and, like so many Christian women in my predicament, trusted that these pastors truly did care for me and already knew how severe the situation had been.

I was categorically wrong.

Their "meeting," for me to "answer a few questions," turned into a two-hour interrogation. Their minds were already made up before I entered the room that *"abuse, even physical abuse, is never biblical grounds for divorce"* (that is a direct quote, with which many Christian counselors and almost *all* pastors I know disagree). It was a horrible experience, in which they tried to back me into the corner using every Scripture possible to convince me that God never permits abuse (even citing Hosea and Gomer as a proof text). The whole "meeting" shocked me – it very much had the feel of asking a rape victim, "Well, how were you dressed at the time of the attack?"

In that two hours of exegetical debate, I cited many verses demonstrating God's protection and provision for the innocent; the marriage contract of Deuteronomy; Paul's principle of abandonment; Jesus' notable refusal to send the woman of John 10 back to her ex-husband(s); Ephesians 4 emphasizing the covenantal importance of husbands loving their wives; and the point of Malachi 2:16 (God's hatred of unjust divorce, where men were treacherously abandoning their wives). Absolutely nothing I said mattered; they told me at the end of the meeting that they did not feel abuse under any circumstances justified divorce. I asked them repeatedly to show me where in the Bible a divorced woman (abused or not) is forced to return to her ex-husband, and they could not.

It's significant that even at that meeting in March 2016, both men A) claimed to believe me; B) claimed to view emotional abuse as just as (if not more) serious than physical abuse, in some cases; and C) are good, seemingly compassionate men who I considered friends. They and their wives had been guests in my home and we were all on friendly terms. I had no reason to believe than anyone had a personal axe to grind against me. I believed, in the words of one counselor, that they were "very well-intentioned, but terribly misguided." Concurrently, I was attending a DivorceCare support group at a neighboring evangelical church, the curriculum of which is taught almost entirely by ACBC and CCEF counselors. The DivoreCare facilitator disagreed not only with my pastor's stance, but also with his use of Matthew 18. Every pastor I knew did.....but none of this mattered.

When Counseling Fails….You Will "Reconcile" Anyway

While the facts of the abuse were not (at least at that point) in dispute, they insisted "reconciliation" was the goal and that I was going to comply. I knew reconciliation was not possible, because my abuser had *said, re-iterated* and *demonstrated* many times in those 20 years that he was not going to repent. This defensive, unrepentant attitude continues to the present day, and he later blamed me – to my face and in front of the children – 100% for his anger problems. He refused to admit he has a serious problem. However, after his anger issues escalated to the point I threatened to divorce him in 2014, he previously did agree that he had been "very emotionally abusive" and we went to biblical counseling together for months to attempt to save the marriage.

Our church had recently gone through a split of sorts and did not have a counseling ministry at the time – all the certified nouthetic counselors except myself, one other woman and a recently ACBC-certified man had left the church, as had both pastors. The current teaching pastor had been there for about two years at that point, but did not do counseling. The counseling pastor, who came in with only two cases of emotional abuse to his experience, had not yet been hired when my then-husband and I finally sought out biblical counseling. I found an ACBC certified counselor in Central Massachusetts, a Presbyterian pastor, and we had a few months' sessions with him. He had our written permission to contact our pastor if he wished. Pastor Mark, our nouthetic counselor from the fall of 2014 until early spring of 2015, recognized the destructive nature of my ex-husband's anger right away. Most of the counseling and homework assignments focused on that.

For a few months things were quieter and more relaxed; then the same old patterns emerged all over again.

A New Nightmare Begins

After the cross-examination with the two pastors, the pressure to "reconcile" started almost immediately. My former husband met with the lead pastor, and professed interest in their counseling process for the sake of the children. He did not deny the fact that he did not love me, and I knew he had no intention of relating to me as a wife. This "process" meant, for them, counseling sessions until the pastors(s) determined my ex-husband was "repentant" and I would then have to move back in with him. Discerning this for the calculated control tactic that it was, I knew the net was tightening. There was too much at stake for me to be allowed to leave.

The same weekend, I asked my former husband over the phone: "Did you actually say that you wanted reconciliation?" In a mocking tone, he replied: "Yes, I did." I asked incredulously, "But why would you say that? You hate me. Did you *tell* him you don't love me?" He laughed, and said, "Hahaha… that never came up!" Then he hung up on me. Later that day, when I went to pick up the kids, he tried to physically intimidate me at the house, and "demanded" I leave the kids at my apartment and "come back here to talk!" I refused, saying, "It's over, buddy. I'm not afraid of you anymore." He didn't like that, and stormed off into the house. I drove immediately to the church, shaking and in tears, and begged the pastor to help me. He promised he would, but never did. The following Sunday, the pastor told me that his conversation with my abuser *"was just to get his perspective on the divorce."*

It was at this point that I started to strongly suspect (and was later proven right) that this whole case was being terribly mishandled. The net effect it had was to justify my ex-husband's attitudes, and to drive our fractured family even further apart. He seemed to find rationalization of his controlling, anger-filled demeanor in the "spiritual head of household" teaching, which he wielded like a club. I had tried every way I knew how to be the godly, submissive wife God had called me to be, in spite of his faults. The more submissive I became, the more abusive my ex-husband became. It was a vicious cycle, which I outlined in great detail in my written statement.

On April 28, 2016 I received a voicemail from the pastor. He urged me to come in for *another* meeting, with himself, the counseling pastor, and my ex-husband so we could "look at the Word of God together." A colleague of mine in the biblical counseling world and I spoke on the phone until late into the night. She told me she had seen this scenario played out many times by pastors who were knowledgeable and caring, but just didn't understand emotional abuse. She offered to speak to the pastor (which she did, and explained to him the lengthy process her center goes through to ensure repentance is genuine – minimum a year, usually longer before any talk of reconciliation occurs). She advised me not to let myself be again put in that situation – the two pastors cornering me (especially with my ex-husband there in the room), because of the obvious power dynamics. I declined the meeting, and my response to the pastor read in part:

As far as meeting again, thank you for your concern (which I am sure is well-intentioned), but I will have to decline your invitation. I've said all I had to say, even coming back and answering your questions when you cross-examined me a few weeks ago. And no; I am *not* returning to my former husband; neither of us wants reconciliation; and [ex-husband] wants "as little communication between [him and me] as possible". So please let's drop this. There is *nothing more to discuss*. Honestly, the best way you could support us right now would be to respect those boundaries. Yes, I assure you I have looked at God's Word quite a bit these years...it has a lot to say about mistreatment of others (esp. those weaker than one's self), unrighteous anger, and abuse of power – including in marriage. Escaping an abuser is *not* sin, and I did not break the marriage covenant by leaving ; my former husband did when he refused to love me and chose to mistreat me. As a trained biblical counselor, I would never try to persuade a woman to return to such a situation.

….. I have carefully documented the years of intimidation which led to the breakdown of the marriage in a seven-page statement, for just such a time. However, after much thought and prayer, I have decided not to send it for two reasons. First, I do not think you are questioning the fact that it was abuse; you have told me that you simply *do not believe that abuse – no matter the type or severity – justifies divorce.* This is where we disagree; therefore, the scope and nature of [ex-husband's] treatment of me is not relevant. Secondly, it would expose him and embarrass him in front of the elders if you chose to share it, and that is not my objective. He is not the one escalating this; we are two mature adults who bi-laterally agreed to the terms of a no-fault divorce, and we need to co-parent in a civil manner. Confessing his sins to church leadership would do nothing to facilitate that; it would simply stir up more 'drama' and cause more relational problems. Pastor, please consider this my final word on the subject. I will not defend or justify myself further.

I did end up having to send the pastor my statement, as the pressure to reconcile continued. While the facts were not contested, they were not considered relevant as the ongoing situation conflicted with the leaders' agenda. Simultaneously, the intimidation by my ex-husband continued; and on May 5th, 2016, two months after our divorce paperwork had been processed by the court, I received another email from the pastor. I was informed that we were both required to be in separate counseling "with the ultimate goal of reconciliation." Of course, Matthew 18 was cited – which I immediately recognized as an ultimatum. Far from being interested in my safety of our family dynamics, the pastor made his agenda clear. *In 3 paragraphs, he used the word "reconcile" or "reconciliation" 14 times.*

While sounding very spiritual on the surface, and making lots of promises, many things horrified me about this email – not the least of which was the implication that my ex-husband was "open to the process of reconciliation". He had made it abundantly clear to me privately that not only was he *not* repentant (or even apologetic) about his treatment of me, and wanted me "as far away from him as possible."

The Toll to My Physical and Spiritual Health

I was already under an enormous amount of stress, and that vaguely threatening message from the pastor caused me to have what I now know was a panic attack at work the next day. It did not require much "reading between the lines" to realize I was being faced with an ultimatum. Even our own children were warning me that returning to him would be the worst possible scenario. There was no way out of this nightmare. Fortunately, I was at work in the hospital at the time.

My heartrate had been accelerated for weeks at that point, as I never knew when the next call or email would come. It became rapid and irregular as I wandered into the cafeteria between interpreting assignments, and I felt like I couldn't breathe. I inhaled as deeply as I could, like a drowning person, and had the sensation that my diaphragm would not expand enough to take in oxygen. My whole body was shaking, and terrified I began crying. From the partial privacy of a booth, I texted my scheduling coordinator:

> I'm sorry Stephanie I am upstairs in the cafeteria......I can't stop crying and I was too embarrassed to come downstairs. There was nobody in the chaplain's office ...I am sorry, I have reached the end of my rope and I don't know if anyone from them can help me. The pastor will not give up, he sent me a long e-mail last night.... they're not even listening to me.......all he keeps yapping about is counseling with the goal of reconciliation in mind and no, I'm never going back to that hellish marriage. He took the house, he took the kids now he's taking the church and of course I should leave; this is horrible......but the kids WON'T leave, so they'll stay there with him and again I lose. Oh God.....I've lost everything and now will lose my ministry as

well because I'll be put out of the church. They are blackmailing me. All because I couldn't take the abuse anymore

I'm sorry...I want to kill myself and I'm here but I can't move. Can you page a chaplain.....maybe they could talk, idk

Stephanie, who by now knew the situation well, arrived in the cafeteria accompanied by a hospital chaplain within minutes. She had been warning me for months that I needed to leave that church for the sake of my own spiritual health and safety. Moreover, she told me repeatedly to get my children as far away from such cult-like teaching as possible. My daughters were being groomed to accept doormats-status (while dressed up in flowery spiritual-sounding language); whereas my sons, whether they ever realize it or not, were being conditioned to see women as second-class citizens in heaven and at home. Although my older son had twice promised me (by text message) that he would never, *ever* treat his future wife the way he witnessed his father treating me, patriarchal teaching in Youth Groups can be subtle enough that the teens don't even spot it as such.

The chaplain described it as "an extremely toxic spiritual environment" and offered to help in any way possible. For the moment, all they could do was stay with me until my breathing stabilized and I calmed down enough to pull myself together. They also referred me to a counselor who specialized in domestic trauma through the hospital's employee assistance program. Unfortunately, with the ongoing harassment escalating, I was experiencing almost all of the symptoms of PTSD. My second panic attack happened in the middle of the night, about a week after the first. Heart racing, I was drenched in sweat and gasping for breath. Since the interference from the pastors had begun, I had lost nearly ten pounds (I am thin to begin with) and was suffering from insomnia. (See chapter 10 for more information about the physical manifestations of ongoing abuse and psychological trauma.) The idea of being forced back into that marriage terrified me, despite how much I missed my children the half-week they lived with their dad.

The Spiritual Coercion Continues

Nevertheless, I did exactly as the pastor demanded – even submitting to counseling with another nouthetic counselor for several months. (This is the only form of Christian counseling my former church deems acceptable.) Rather than focus on the trauma of my marriage and healing from the severe effects of PTSD I was suffering, the counselor and I did a Bible study on the Beatitudes. The pastor's agenda was for the counselor to groom me to return to my ex-husband at some indeterminate date. On May 18th 2016, knowing how traumatized and fragile I was, my former pastor wrote in an email to me that counseling was *"Not simply with the goal of healing from the pain of the past, but with the ultimate goal of reconciliation in the future."* It was at that moment that I knew, beyond any doubt, that this pastor cared nothing whatsoever about me as a human being. All that seemed to matter was his agenda – even if people's lives were destroyed in the process.

The nouthetic counselor with whom I met was reluctant to push for a "reconciliation at all costs" agenda; not sure at all that was God's will. She explained her reservations to the pastor, and that her focus was to be strictly on my relationship with God. He agreed, and in fact I wrote a number of blog posts reflecting on the Beatitudes during that time. (The counselor, who had left our church during an earlier church split, privately expressed concern to me about the "inconsistent way the church handles divorces," even citing her own brother, a long-time member in good standing who had been divorced and re-married twice while there and the fact that leadership never raised an eyebrow.)

Broken Promises

A male member of the church and good friend (who is extremely adept theologically) read the pastor's demands of me and offered to speak to him on my behalf. His initial comment was "They're doing 'Matthew 18' on the wrong spouse here, Marie." One of my first defenders, he and his wife read all the coercive emails as they came in, and supported me through the ordeal. Later, other church members came forward telling me they disagreed with the church leadership's stance on abuse and divorce generally, and their treatment of me personally.

The same month, May 2016, the pastor and I did have a lengthy and seemingly-positive conversation by phone, in which I was able to explain more characteristics of the pattern and nature of the abuse. My main concern, which he agreed was perfectly valid, was how the pastors and elders were going to be able to gauge repentance and not be fooled by my ex-husband just saying the right words and doing the merry-go-round of counseling again. The testimony of our four kids also supported my claims of ongoing mistreatment/manipulation. We set two conditions to any talks of "reconciliation," to which he agreed: unambiguous repentance; and a full physical and psychiatric evaluation prior to any nouthetic counseling commencing. The pastor heartily agreed to the necessity of both of these terms, and also assured me that this was going to be a very lengthy process whereby no talk of reconciliation would happen under any circumstances for *at least* a year.

Neither condition was ever met, and the pastor again broke his promise to me.

Ten weeks (less than three months) later, I received another email from the pastor, asking me where we were in the "reconciliation process" and what 'growth and change' I'd seen in my ex-husband. I was shocked. Weeks earlier, in July 2016, I had documented ongoing mistreatment that had continued since the separation (including dates, specific statements, vindictive things done and said to and about me, and sources). When pressed about "reconciliation," mere weeks after receiving these pleas for help from myself and my adult daughter, I responded in a very lengthy and detailed email (attaching two pages of testimony from the kids). It was ignored.

And yet the pastor wanted *me* in counseling, "to deal with [my] sinful reactions to [ex-husband's] behavior." I believe now, as I did then, that the only "sinful" response to abuse is *no* response.

Divorce had clearly been the correct and only decision in my case. I had ample biblical grounds; nothing was ever going to change, and the unfolding events of the spring and summer of 2016 bore witness to that. I considered myself vindicated, as did those close to me who witnessed what was going on. In early August 2016, the pastor preached a sermon on divorce that concerned a number of people in the church, including my daughter who texted me her concerns about the way women were "being given the short end of the stick." He stated plainly that abuse is not valid grounds for divorce (his theology allows for separation but not divorce, a position which we discussed in chapter 3). Based upon his unyielding, merciless ultimatum to abused wives, the complete lack of assistance or protection I received from the church, and his continual pressure on me to "reconcile" while conveniently overlooking my abuser's refusal to acknowledge his treatment of me, I knew there was no hope for resolution. In one of the most painful decisions of my life, I realized I could no longer stay in the church I had called "family" for over a decade.

The Resignation

Following two more increasingly coercive emails (in the early autumn of 2016) from the pastors, demanding additional "meetings" to discuss "hard things" and imminent reconciliation, I sent my former church's board of elders a certified, legal letter of resignation. (I had not attended their church in almost two months at that point, but they evidently hadn't noticed.) God had graciously led strong Christian leaders and friends to minister to me during this horrible time, which I will discuss later in the chapters on healing. Refusing to accept my resignation, on October 14th, 2015 I received yet another email, this one from the board of elders. (Later, other former members of the church emailed me their "letters", in which entire sentences and paragraphs were identical. Evidently, the church used a copy-paste template when excoriating former parishioners.) The letter stated that "the covenant you entered into when you became a church member does not allow for resignation in circumstances such as these." Heavily threatening in its tone, the letter implied that I could expect more and escalated harassment if I did not acquiesce to their demands and repent of my supposed "sinful response" to the abuse. In a paragraph dripping with condescension, I was informed that in "marital cases where there is bi-lateral sin, it is not uncommon for the spouse who has been wronged [note: not abused] to feel that he/she is being blamed."

The word choice of "bilateral sin" and emphasizing my supposed "sinful response" to the abuse was telling, as was their insistence that I would not be permitted to leave under "circumstances such as these." Interestingly, they never clarified exactly what "circumstances" those would be. A wife flees an abusive 20-year marriage, only to be told she "isn't permitted" to leave a church she has already left?

Victim-Blaming as "Counsel"

When a board of elders or individual pastor sends a woman a letter such as this, implying that she, the victim, is somehow partially at fault for her own mistreatment, and refusing to accept her official resignation from their church, they seem to be counting on two things: A) that the woman doesn't know Scripture sufficiently well to defend herself; and B) that she doesn't know the law of the land well enough to defend herself. Fortunately, I was well-acquainted with both.

Trying to implicate the recipient of someone else's sin against her as being (even partially) responsible is, of course, completely unbiblical. This is not to say that I am perfect or without sin; nor do I claim to have been a faultless wife. I realize full well that I made mistakes in our marriage, but that in no way is to say that I was responsible for the anger and turbulence that destroyed it. Nor does it provide an argument to return to a situation where I have only been promised more of the same. On October 7th, one week before I received this message, my former husband entrapped me outside his office and told me that I not only "deserved all that and more" because I "wasn't submissive enough," but that his mistreatment of me had not been abuse, and that I had "a problem with authority." With a gleam in his eye, he assured me that one day I would go to hell because Ephesians 5:22 ("Wives submit to your husbands") comes *before* the verses about husbands loving their wives. Therefore, he reasoned, it was incumbent upon me to submit without question to every form of treatment he could dish out, before he was required to love me. Thus, I was at fault for his explosive anger and abusive rages – despite the fact I had "submitted" to the point of becoming a quivering shell of a woman.

Sickened, I could not imagine how he was able to pull off the "repentance act" in front of the pastors, but their condescending letter to me a week after this incident trying to "victim-shame" me was too much. Saddened that I had been re-victimized by the very men in authority who had promised to help me, I at least realized that I had legal recourse as a non-member of their church.

The Church is Subject to the Law of the Land

In the United States, an individual has the right to leave a voluntary organization (including a religious organization, such as a church) at will. The types of churches that typically employ their "discipline" proceedings in all cases of divorce also routinely write clauses into their bylaws, prohibiting members from resigning while they are "under church discipline." The notion of being "under church discipline" is a rather subjective one in many cases, which leaders may twist and yield to their advantage (or to suit their agenda). Realizing I had left an abusive marriage, the initial emails cajoling me to participate in the 'reconciliation process' stated that my former husband was the one "under church discipline." However, as the abuse continued and I scrupulously documented it – refusing to discuss "reconciliation" until a few terms had been met – suddenly *I* was the one "under church discipline." Why? Because patriarchal church leaders aren't used to women standing up for themselves.

Regardless of how leaders may construe or wrongly implement their "discipline" proceedings, what they are counting on is their congregation's ignorance that *such clauses are illegal*. Regardless of how a church tries to prevent a member from leaving in its bylaws or membership covenant, such a clause is not recognized by a court of law, and is considered coercion. Very few members of such high-control religious groups know that obstructing their resignation is against the law.

No matter how churches may spiritualize "pursuit of errant [in their view] sheep," they are also violating biblical principles. The Church is bound by the governing authorities (Romans 13:1-7; Titus 3:1; 1 Peter 2:13-14), which in this case means federal law and the authority of the Commonwealth of Massachusetts. They have no authority to continue to claim a former member who has officially tendered a resignation as part of their own, nor to use their internal "discipline proceedings" to silence her. When they attempt to do so, it is considered defamation. A 1984 case in which a Florida woman sued her former church for defamation (she was denounced in a church-wide meeting days after submitting her resignation) resulted in a $390,000 award for the plaintiff. The case, *Guinn v. Church of Christ Collinsville* was upheld even after appeal, because the church's actions were well outside of First Amendment protection (which deals with matters of religious liberty). The court held that binding commitments to a church had no effect in law:

> ...All religious activity in the United States is consensual, a person who publically claims not to be a member of a church is legally not a member of that church and church discipline cannot continue without consent. A church attempting to discipline a person that has withdrawn can be found to be engaging in a form of harassment.[43]

Using coercion and threats of humiliation (before the congregation) for resigning is a cultic method of control. While my former church does not meet all of the criteria for a "cult," in that they are not preaching rank heresy, one of the marks of a cult is, in fact, the practice of pursuing and defaming members who leave. If they cannot get away with doing so publically, they will try privately using more covert methods of defamation. Months after the media covered my story and the church was forced to accept my resignation, my former pastor was still trying desperately to control the narrative – even sending friends of mine messages on Facebook, inviting them to have "conversations" about me with him.

Are Church "Membership Covenants" Mentioned in the Bible?

One of the "trump cards" authoritarian churches use to prevent members from leaving is the 'membership covenant' he or she has voluntarily signed. Typically, clauses forbidding members from leaving the congregation in cases of mistreatment are absent from the "covenant" itself, more typically hidden somewhere in the bylaws (which few prospective members take the time to read). The membership covenant usually contains the church's Statement of Faith, and asks prospective members to participate in church life under the authority of its leaders. It all sounds very benign on the surface, but is this practice biblical?

---

[43] http://church-discipline.blogspot.com/2008/01/marian-guinn-vs-church-of-christ.html

Scripture is full of references to covenants – more than mere agreements, the covenantal bond includes binding promises from God to man; man to God; and between individuals. The Bible describes five separate covenants made between God and His people in the Old Testament. Examples of human covenants would include David's to Jonathan (1 Samuel 18:3) and Abraham and Abimelech, the king of the Philistines (Genesis 21). Yet oddly enough, for all of the emphasis on membership covenants in churches that profess to be sola-Scriptura, the practice is never mentioned in the New Testament. In the Early Church, a person's inclusion into the Church was by believer's baptism. A profession of faith in Christ was a pre-requisite to being considered part of His Body, and baptism was considered the outward sign of the "New Covenant" mentioned in Hebrews 8:6-13. The covenant is between the believer and God. *Nowhere* does Scripture mention a covenant between the believer and a local church congregation. This is an unbiblical and cultic practice.

One woman who survived an abusive marriage (and subsequent excommunication of her church) wrote to me:

> I will never sign a "membership covenant" with any church again. It is used as a weapon for cultish control that ignores the work of the Holy Spirit in individual lives. I've heard from *hundreds* of women who have been policed and shunned by their churches when they have had to break their covenant with humans in order to obey God and maintain good conscience before Him. It's not right.

No one in the Early Church was required to sign a written document pledging loyalty or continued membership in a particular local church congregation, and we may surmise that the Apostolic Fathers would have been appalled by such a practice. The Early Christians pledged their life and loyalty to Christ alone, and not a set of laws or regulations conceived by men. Furthermore, the Book of Acts recounts numerous instances of churches being destroyed; disputes arising between believers that caused them to part ways for a time (notably Paul and Barnabas, recorded in Acts 15:36-41); and people planting new churches. Therefore, we may reasonably assume that leaving a local church (for whatever reason) and choosing to seek fellowship in a different Gospel-preaching congregation is not inherently sinful. Much like infant baptism and confession in the Roman Catholic church, the modern practice of pressuring prospective members to sign written "covenants" in conservative evangelical camps is simply a way of exerting control over congregants and keeping them in the flock (where their tithe money and offerings will go), hedging that the vast majority of the sheep will never question the practice and will never realize their spiritual leaders are using a tactic that is neither lawful, *nor* biblical.

When the elders of my former church ignored my official resignation and continued to "pursue" me, my attorney became involved. He sent a second cease-and-desist letter, as the first one had been part of my legal letter of resignation. After refusing to accept my resignation and the injunction to stop contacting me, the pastor had already broken the law and was guilty of harassment, but I still chose not to take legal action against him. Little did I know then this had happened before, and he had ignored multiple warnings that he was going to damage the church's reputation if he continued to harass former members in this way. Sadly, this practice is becoming so common in some branches of American evangelicalism that thousands of women have come forward with their testimonies of secondary abuse from churches – a phenomenon we will look at more closely in the next chapter, as I found resolution to my ordeal.

CHAPTER 9

"Letters" and Kangaroo Courts – More Women Come Forward

"Marie!! I just read your story about the abuse, divorce and the church. The same thing happened to me!!!!! It was terrible and I wound up in a total spiritual crisis over it. I am sad it happened to you too but thankful I'm not alone...They had the elders calling and texting...the pastor told me they were going to present me to the congregation and ask everyone to approach me as an unbeliever...I cited laws and they wrote back immediately refuting the legal things I cited...It was like they already had been through it. It didn't take them but 20 minutes to write back to me refuting it...my ex even told them to stop. It was crazy."
– Testimony of another abuse survivor from my former church

During the ten months I was harassed by the leadership of my former church, I became aware through other Christian authors writing on the subject of abuse and survivor advocate ministries that my story was far from unique. Darlene Parsons, who writes the North Carolina-based blog "The Wartburg Watch," told my local newspaper that my experience was similar to what has happened to many women who belong to Neo-Calvinist, nondenominational evangelical churches that take a rigid stance against divorce. This is the case, she confirmed, even when women have been in abusive marriages. She started her blog after noticing an increase in women being pressured into reconciling with abusive husbands by their evangelical churches, and has seen this grow as a national trend over the past decade. "It's like we opened up a blister, and we're getting story after story. I'm frankly shocked," she said. "I would say that I'm getting word of new stories once a week, (from churches across the country) and they're all tied to this Neo-Calvinist movement that's become more popular."

Because of this movement's telescopic rendering of certain scriptural passages, and their emphasis on complete control of their congregants (especially women), the pastors that endorse this orthopraxy appear to operate from a playbook. Following the legal cease-and-desist order that my attorney sent my former pastor on October 18, 2016, on December 5th I received (via email) a 4-page indictment on official church letterhead. This letter contained numerous lies. Its author twisted incidents and misconstrued statements, finally accusing me of 'slander' and an 'unbiblical divorce'. The last few paragraphs chastised me for my 'sinful choices' (no mention made of the perpetrator's unrepentance, or pages of documentation I had provided) and threatened to hold a meeting with "immediate church membership" to "share details of my sinful choices so they might pray for and pursue me". In expertly-crafted spiritual language, these men were blackmailing me by promising a shameful excommunication if I did not 'repent' and come back.[44]

All for leaving a hopelessly abusive marriage, and making the mistake of coming to them for help.

By this time, however, I not only knew they were operating outside of the law – I knew they had done this to other women. Darlene from The Wartburg Watch, the online ministry mentioned above devoted to exposing spiritually abusive practices and leaders, contacted me for an interview within a week of my receiving that threatening letter. (Apparently, someone from the church was making phone calls to try and discredit me in the biblical counseling world and it backfired – a ministry colleague tipped off the press as to what was actually happening in my quiet, suburban Massachusetts church.)

When the first part of my story was published, other women started coming forward. This had the side-effect of my former church being criticized openly on social media. Within minutes of publication of the second part of

---

[44]   In 2015, Karen Hinkley endured a similar experience under Pastor Matt Chandler at The Village Church in Texas. After her husband was exposed as a pedophile, Karen had the marriage annulled. Leaders at the church claimed he was "walking in repentance" and tried to manipulate Karen into staying in the marriage. When she refused, they threatened to place her under "church discipline"; harassed her with texts round the clock; and invoked her 'membership covenant' when she left for another state. With the ex-husband enjoying church protection while Karen was tormented, the case went viral and the church very narrowly avoided a lawsuit when leaders "released" Karen and flew out to her new city to apologize to her. The case brought widespread attention to the unbiblical nature and illegality of some types of "membership covenants."

the story (dealing with the church's final letter blackmailing me to "repent" or face public defamation, which The Wartburg Watch published in its entirety), both of my former pastors' Twitter accounts disappeared. Hours later, with all the negative publicity, the church's Facebook page and Twitter accounts were also deleted. People across the country were leaving negative reviews of the church on Yelp and their website, which the administrators removed as they came in.

Two weeks later, my story was in the local newspaper. My former pastor and his backup of elders had opened a Pandora's Box that they could not shut again.

The Testimony of Other Victims

Over the years, there have been many divorces at my former church (for different reasons), and consistently it was the *women* who were pressured to reconcile. When they refused, they were sent an official letter like mine putting them out of the church. This has happened so many times that it has become standard operating procedure. I learned that there were secret meetings with hand-picked church members speaking against them, and no matter what the women (in abuse cases) produced as evidence, the husbands were always believed (and in some cases, stay in the church to this day). I know two of the women personally who had to leave – the abusive husbands still managed to convince the elders they were innocent. One woman went to them, police report in hand, and was still told that biblically she had no choice but to "reconcile." Like me, she refused – and was put out of the church. I simply left on my own initiative, knowing I was 100% in the right.

After my story became public, another woman from my former church came forward with a similar story of harassment because her divorce was deemed "unbibical":

My story is far less extensive than Marie's but mirrors it in some regard. Some time ago my husband and I separated. We had been attending [church's name redacted] for approximately nine or ten years. Looking back, I am horrified that I received far more communication going through a divorce than I did when I struggled with infertility and subsequently delivered premature twins who then passed away shortly after birth. *One* person from that church made the trip to Boston to express condolences and see how I was doing, and it was a friend of mine who was a non-elder/non-leader of the church. The pastor at the time *never* visited. Even after we were home. Anyhow I digress ...

My husband and I separated due to his verbal abuse. After taking the abuse and control for several years, I built a wall and finally asked my husband to leave. He went to the pastor for counsel, who then began calling and texting me with regard to my *"moving forward with an unbiblical divorce."*

Shortly thereafter, my husband, upon receiving counsel from others, arrived home one day and announced that he was "not leaving" because I "could not ask him to leave or make him move out since this was his home." I immediately left and proceeded to lease a house nearby. We arranged a custody schedule that was suitable to both of us and our children.

The pastor contacted me a few times attempting to persuade me to meet with him to discuss the situation and to reconcile with my husband. Instead of meeting with him, I sought outside Christian couples counseling. Not only that, my husband and I both had individual counseling.

The pastor let me know that if I proceeded with this "unbiblical" divorce he would present me to the church membership as an unbeliever and ask them to approach me as such. I was appalled and deeply hurt! My faith in the church was tested and I wavered more. I felt as if I bore a scarlet letter among my friends who largely attended there. (Turns out they were supportive.)

I sent the church a letter stating that I was resigning my membership and therefore, releasing them from any obligation to hold me accountable (i.e. continuing the barrage of communication). Following the letter, I continued to receive communication. At this point, my estranged husband felt compelled to contact the pastor, urging him to please leave me alone and forego his plan to "tell it to the congregation." My husband reported back to me that the pastor responded by saying he "had to" continue. Why? Because I was a member of the "universal church" and therefore he was still obligated to proceed with the accountability measures.

At this point I emailed the pastor and demanded that he stop the communication or I would take legal action. Following all that, I had great anxiety that someone was going to show up at my door. I also blocked the phone numbers of the pastor as well as the elders. When a friend from the church contacted me, I always began the conversation by asking whether they were contacting me of their own accord or because the church had asked them to call. It was such an anxiety-ridden period of time!

A few months later, my husband and I reconciled for a period of time. At that point we both stopped attending that church and found another one. The calls and contacts had stopped – I assume because we had gotten back together. Because I had blocked the calls months earlier, I had no way of knowing whether communication from that church was attempted or not. I never agreed to meet with anyone at any time from there.

Several months later, my husband and I separated once again and the dissolution of our marriage did take place. We never received any communication from the church we were attending regarding our divorce. My ex-husband still attends the church we found together, and I have found a new church.

I think one reason the Church, this church in particular, takes such a strong stand on this divorce thing is because it's one of the only tangible "sins" they can wrap their heads around and actually hold people accountable for. You can't go into somebody's bedroom and see their pornography, you can't control the abusive family member, you can't measure the amount of gossip that ensues through a church, etc. It's sickening though. I literally felt like I had a scarlet letter, and sometimes I still do. They really get into your head with messed up information based on Scripture taken out of context.

Finally, it cannot be overstated that the men at our former church have totally bought into the modus operandi as well. My ex-husband for example, still attempts to control every situation he is involved in with me and the kids.

A History of Injustice

This woman, who had been harassed throughout 2014, had even saved screenshots of the emails from our former pastor. They were eerily similar to the covertly-aggressive messages I had received from him, although she was given a deadline of six months to move back in with her ex-husband whereas I was never quoted an exact timeline. (Perhaps this is due to the fact that I halted the process as soon as I realized their 'reconciliation' plan was unconditional.)

A former elder told me that he had stood up at an elders' meeting in 2014 and defended this woman, trying to warn the pastor: "If a former member is even *implying* harassment, you need to back off. This will do great damage to the church's reputation in the community!" While several deacons and at least one elder expressed a desire to compassionately help wives who had been abused, so many of us received what came to be called "The Letter" that it appeared to be standard operating procedure. When a woman produces a police report on her ex-husband for operating under the influence; documents multiple cases of abuse and the fact he totaled his car while drunk, she should not be urged to "go on a date with him." When men with serious, unaddressed anger issues proclaim that they will never change their ways – and after decades of torment their wives take them at their word – the wives are not the ones who should be painted as having "hardened hearts". This elder, and several deacons, subsequently left the church as they were unable to communicate what godly leadership looks like to the pastor.

Another woman (not divorced) left because the former counseling pastor was teaching in an adult Sunday school class that *even if a woman is being beaten*, she cannot divorce her husband. A long-time church member then stood up and gave examples of when it might be "acceptable" to slap one's wife. A furor resulted, and the senior pastor (now retired) tried to do damage control although several people still fled. These were not recent events, but allegedly there is a long history of marital abuse being swept under the rug at our former church with the onus for "reconciliation" (at all costs) being put on the women.

Standing My Ground and Defense Before the Trial Court

After the elders gave me an "ultimatum" date of December 23, 2016 to return to reconciliation talks at their church (or face public shaming) and The Wartburg Watch covered the story, several media outlets around the country and a few defamation lawyers took notice. Even absent the media coverage and private support I received, I had no intention of backing down. On the contrary, I was already seeing my ministry become more effective: other Christian women in abusive marriages were coming to me for counsel and help. At Christmastime, my father (a retired history teacher) slipped me a handwritten note, in which he quoted Martin Luther and exhorted me to "stand [my] ground." Countless women (and at least a few men) from my former church also called and emailed me their support, knowing much of what I had endured.

Unlike many abused wives (and former wives), I was blessed to have the leadership at my new church standing up for me as well. Unbeknownst to me, while the media attention and potential legal action was heating up, my new spiritual mentors were meeting and corresponding with my former pastor in attempt to help him realize how un-Christ-like and damaging his course of action was. With much prayer and great patience, they tried to reason with him. In a lengthy letter, one of the leaders of my current church exhorted my former pastor to recognize that I was no longer under his spiritual leadership, but theirs; and as such, his pursuit of me was, indeed, harassment. The issue of "disciplining" the victim of domestic abuse was also addressed:

> **...the particulars of this situation between Marie and [ex-husband] is deeply complex, involving various forms of hard-to-define abuse.** It is naive for either you or I as men to think we can grasp the vulnerability, violation, and trauma of abuse, no matter its form, that can be instigated by a husband to his wife. And, even if one disavows the idea that abuse is ever a possible biblical ground for divorce (a perspective of which I would tread on very cautiously exegetically), any public discussion of "unrepentant sin" in this situation should not focus on just one party. Singling out Marie for public discipline to the exclusion of [ex-husband] is simply not consistent with the totality of the situation (Col 3:19, Ps 11:5, Ep 4:29-32, Ep 5:25-33, Ep 6:4).

> **...if one is to follow Matt 18 by its spirit, then its end goal must be restoration, pure and simple.** However, we don't believe that your planned course of action is restorative, given the specific nature of these circumstances. In fact, we believe it would be highly damaging and traumatic to Marie spiritually, emotionally, and relationally (with her children) if you continue in your escalation proceedings. Throughout the gospels, Jesus came down hardest on those who focused on the letter of the law instead of the spirit of the law (Mt 23:23). Playing this situation "by the book" with no regard for the delicacy, grayness, and complexities of the situation is simply not consistent with the ministry of our Savior (Mt 12:9-13)....people's spiritual and relational lives are at stake here – it's not something that should be carried out as a sterile, legal procedure. In the end, Marie is deeply wounded and needs a safe haven in which she can heal and nourish her faith, not a trial court to be rushed before (Jn 8:1-11).

> **...we are seeking to provide a safe haven and be a comfort to Marie** (Ps 27:4-5, Is 24:4). We also seek to shepherd her, help her understand how her Christian faith plays out in her life decisions, and encourage her to flee from sin in all its forms (Heb 12:1) as we are transformed more and more into the likeness and image

of Jesus Christ (2 Cor 5:17). We believe she is trying to seek and find the Lord in the midst of a brutally tough, life-changing situation; during our interactions with Marie, we have found no grounds to believe that she is flagrantly fleeing or rebelling against God in this process (Jer 30:15).

Notwithstanding all the support I received from so many strong Christians, a few were incensed that I had had the audacity to stand up to the abuse – first marital; and then spiritual. One female nouthetic counselor, who had never met me in person, sent me a vitriolic email demanding that I "repent" for speaking out and "return to Christ." I cannot "return" to Christ, as I have never left Him. Repent for standing up for myself? For refusing to endure additional torment (either from my former husband, or his church leaders)? Repent of taking a stand against spiritual abuse, so that (Lord willing) other women won't have to? Several pastors assured me this was common backlash – that there are many within the visible Church who believe exposing spiritual abuse to be a far greater wrong than the abuse itself.

In January 2017, with increased focus from the media, steadfast pressure from leaders at my current church, and the possibility of a class-action lawsuit hanging over their heads, my former church relented and sent me another letter – one paragraph – agreeing to accept my resignation from membership, "with great sadness and heaviness of heart." Legally, they were in the clear. I did not press charges; and, although it saddened me greatly to see my children continue to attend this church, I allowed them their choice in the matter. (Understandably, they wanted to stay where their friends attend – as most teens and pre-teens would.) I can only continue to pray for them and hope that they will discern the difference between true, complementarian teaching from the Bible – and the patriarchal authoritarian system that enslaves and silences women.

Sometimes Supportive.....but Not Always Competent to Counsel

It is evident by the very fact that there is dispute over these proceedings that most Christian churches *do* seek to help and support women who have dealt with mistreatment (both domestic, and subsequent spiritual abuse). We cannot make a blanket statement and say "the Church does not care about the plight of abused women." This is simply not true. Many churches, while supportive of women in cases of abuse and adultery, simply don't know what to do.

Well-intentioned pastors sometimes send women for "counsel" which may do more harm than good – very few in the Church seem to understand the inner-workings and mindset of abusive men. (The counseling pastor at my former church, who was meeting with my ex-husband, admitted to me at the very beginning that he had only counseled two cases of emotional abuse beforehand.) And yet, as an ACBC-certified counselor, he was the only one deemed appropriate to counsel chronically abusive men.

Other women whose churches have taken a less-didactic approach to dealing with separation from abusers have also testified to the lack of knowledge and experience in counseling these men. "Ashley" from the Midwest writes about her experience in a church that ultimately supported her in separating from her abuser, but didn't really know how to help:

> In August 2012 my marriage blew up. I discovered that my husband of 11 years had been having numerous extramarital affairs and had a massive porn addiction. My church (of the denomination Presbyterian Church in American, or PCA) was extremely supportive – but that comes with the caveat that I had approached our former pastor with emails my then-husband had been exchanging with a woman from another state about meeting up for a weekend rendezvous. The pastor seemed concerned, but then just told my husband to buy me flowers and say "I'm sorry." Turns out the pastor himself was involved in several affairs in the community and we only found out when he moved away and women started coming forward. So, naturally he was not committed to helping me when he was deeply involved in his own sin.
>
> My church was supportive and put together a plan – my husband and I separated (briefly), we had in-church counseling with a pastoral care counselor, we were sent to a Biblical Intensive Counseling session out of state. Additionally, my ex had accountability partners set up. The Intensive Counseling had some extensive "homework" involved after the session (15-16 weeks, to be exact) that we were supposed to complete. I was diligently doing the work, reading the books and going through the necessary items involved. My husband made a few grand gestures to make it look like he was repentant and would do all that was required of him, but he quickly fell off the bandwagon and blamed me for it. He shrugged off all accountability from the church (to the point where the pastor and elders asked me if he changed his number, because he never returned their calls or texts) and kept telling me it was my fault. I just needed to "forgive him, trust him and shut up about it already."

The homework from Intensive Counseling was particularly damaging. We read a lot of John Piper and others who were basically saying that marriage is for life; God condemns divorce for *any* reason; and that women should persevere. The "permanence view" was so difficult to adhere to. I had always known that God allows divorce for adultery; so why was this man (Piper) saying it wasn't ok to divorce for that reason? Around that time, God opened my eyes to a lot of things (namely, the severe emotional abuse I also suffered at the hands of this man) and brought me to many good resources such *A Cry for Justice* by Jeff Crippen. That was instrumental in my learning, growth and courage.

The church was understanding with me. The new pastor and elders met with me over the next two and a half years as I sought to do the hard work of reconciliation, alone. They heard my anguished cries. They saw how my ex-husband was not truly repentant and wanted to *say* the right things, but actions never followed. We were not fooled. They helped me get a lawyer and get strong legal counsel. They assisted me financially when he would not pay the bills. They had men go to the house after I told my ex-husband that I had filed for divorce and wanted him out of the house. I had a great group of women around me who loved, prayed for and supported me in my very dark days.

One thing I would say the church didn't get right is how to *spiritually* support a single mom. I attended a small church and there were no other single or divorced moms. It was lonely and awkward. They weren't sure how to support me (besides financially and with prayer). I needed practical help with my home, with my kids, packing to move, etc. I was finally forced to ask for very specific things, which felt strange and "too needy." I did eventually get the help I needed, which was good because I really had to get packed up and have the yard ready.

I think another thing that I struggle with is the fact that, after I found out about the depth of my ex's sexual addiction and years of cheating, I shouldn't have been given a timetable of when he needed to move back in. That put so *much* pressure squarely on me. I remember the pastoral care counselor saying it could be "no more than four months" of separation before my husband moved back in, and that was even too long in his mind because he had one couple that was separated for 4 months who couldn't reconcile. I think it should be an open-ended arrangement. I felt a lot of pressure to allow him back in the home and we had not rebuilt trust at all. I think things would have ended more quickly because I would have seen that he wasn't doing the work necessary and wasn't truly repentant. Letting him back in the home, with the kids, was extremely hard, because subsequently they really struggled when we split for good.

Well-intentioned (but Misguided) Advice

While not entirely positive, "Ashley's" experience was less heavy-handed than that of many women in conservative evangelical and/or Reformed churches. Increasingly, Gospel-preaching churches are becoming more aware of the problem of domestic abuse and are concerned for the victims, but don't quite know how to respond to the problem. The pat answer seems to be to fall back on nouthetic counseling, which is not always helpful (especially when the counselor is neither experienced nor knowledgeable about the unique psychology that drives abusers' mentality and behavior).

Emotional abuse is certainly harder to define than physical abuse, and cannot always be pin-pointed to a certain set of behaviors – although set patterns will emerge in abusive relationships. Because of this ambiguity, the counselor's (or pastor's) job is not an easy one. In order to change behaviors, speech, and attitudes, they must be specifically confronted. And emotional abuse cannot be effectively confronted if the counselor doesn't understand what it is.

The following illustration, excerpted from "The Silent Killer of Christian Marriages" illustrates this difficulty well:

> Erica desperately wanted out of her marriage with Jack, but she could not connect her feelings of despair and an almost overpowering desire to escape with anything overtly destructive Jack was doing. Jack was a good father, had no problem with alcohol or drugs, did not chase other women, was a good provider, and had never harmed her physically. By contrast, Erica was aware of her own shortcomings as a wife and mother. She experienced guilt, feelings of inadequacy, and embarrassment over her inability to respond sexually to her husband.
>
> Frequently, this is the presenting picture of a woman in an emotionally abusive marriage. In the absence of physical abuse, neither the woman nor the pastor she seeks out for help is

likely to recognize that the emotional climate of the marriage is squeezing the life out of her.

> There is little room for disagreement over what constitutes physical abuse, and its damaging or even lethal potential is recognized by almost everyone. The nature and impact of emotional abuse, however, is not so easily nor widely recognized. Although the signs of emotional abuse are not always clear, the abuser's behavior is not obvious, and the immediate results are not dramatic as in physical abuse, emotional abuse represents an oppressive and insidious process that strikes deeply at the hearts of its victims.[45]

In a constant climate of destructive criticism, intimidation, and other forms of abuse we have discussed, a woman feels that she has no choices and no hope for a way out. It is very difficult to adequately convey these feelings and document every abusive incident or statement for someone outside the marriage whom she may perceive to be standing in judgement of her. Although she knows she is in a destructive relationship, she may fear reprisals if she stands up – and victim-blaming if she speaks out. It is often easier for an abused women to say nothing than to risk having her situation badly mishandled by attempting to share with her spiritual advisors.

Another factor that sometimes prevents well-meaning pastors from being able to address marital abuse effectively is that of *culture*. Some cultural groups hold to a more patriarchal worldview, which, while not inherently abusive, can be used to dismiss or minimize verbal or emotional abuse of their wives. Lundy Bancroft even cites different types of abuse more likely to surface among certain ethnic groups than others, based on his decades of experience counseling abusive men. (For example, jealousy and accusations of infidelity seem to be more common among Latino populations, although the men will tolerate more "back-talk" from women; whereas white abusers tend to have very strict "rules" about how a woman may argue or stand up for herself in an argument.) I will address the issue of cultural differences more thoroughly in Chapter 12, when we examine how the Church may better address issues of abuse that arise in her midst.

The Truth that Frees Us

When standing up for truth is seen as unloving; when victims are coerced into apologizing to their abusers; when sincere believers blindly follow their

---

45 Amy Wildman White, "The Silent Killer of Christian Marriages," excerpted from *Healing the Hurting* (Catherine Clark Kroeger and James R. Beck, editors; Ada: Baker Book House Company, 1998).

leaders spinning their version of a story at the expense of an individual, there is a serious problem in the Body. Although I am still in the early phases of healing from spiritual abuse, my dismay and powerlessness was the catalyst to reach out to others with similar stories and to speak out.

Given the prevalence of such unjust proceedings against abused women in the evangelical church, we must now turn to the most important part of this book – how does a woman find hope, when her own church leaders betray her? Will she ever heal, not only from the wounds inflicted by the man she pledged to love and honor "til death do us part," but from Christ's Church itself? How can she maintain her faith amidst such obstacles? And finally, how can the Church better serve these vulnerable women, while remaining true to the Gospel?

In the next chapter, I will discuss my own healing journey and that of other women in similar situations. While everyone's journey is different, there are timeless principles and immutable truth with which God has blessed His daughters. His love, grace and truth alone will lead us out of the wilderness.

CHAPTER 10

Where Does Healing Begin?

"Are you going to care for the opinion of men here, or
for the opinion of God? The opinion of men won't avail us
much when we get before the judgment throne."
– Charles Studd, 19th Century British missionary

Recovering from the trauma of domestic abuse takes time. Just as every survivor's story is different, people grieve (the loss of dreams; the loss of dignity; the attack on their own personhood) differently. Recovering one's sense of self and trust in God can be excruciatingly slow. There are often setbacks (including secondary abuse from clergy, as we have already seen) that will make the healing process much lengthier, but God is faithful and will never abandon His own (Deuteronomy 31:6-8; Psalm 94:14).

My Own Healing Journey

For me, healing began at a summer camp in a remote part of Albania.

Six months after my divorce, I was on a mission trip at a summer camp for teens in Albania. I had recently begun attending another local church where close friends of mine worship, and had planned this trip for months as a time to serve and be spiritually renewed myself. I was unable to heal while still attending my former church, where I had to see my ex-husband every week and be constantly pressured by the leadership to "reconcile." The new church was planted by a compassionate and exegetically knowledgeable pastor, who was very familiar with my case and that of several other women who had been through similar ordeals.

While dear friends from another church brought me to retreats, Bible studies, and spent many hours talking and praying with me, the hurt inflicted by those whose opinions I judged "significant"made me ambivalent towards God – all while serving Him in ministry. I looked forward to August 2016, a month I had set aside to serve at Youth Camps (in New Hampshire as well as the one in Albania); spend time with my children, and heal. One of the things I most looked forward to in Albania was seeing precious brothers and sisters in Christ whom I had befriended at camp years prior. I "needed" them – needed their presence; needed their friendship; needed to laugh.

Finding God on the Ionian Coast

After three days in Tirana, I boarded a bus to the southern city of Saranda where I would be met and taken to camp. Most of the staff with whom I was closest did not attend camp that year for a variety of reasons. Surrounded by unfamiliar young campers, new staff, and total immersion in Albanian, I felt much more alone than I ever had at camp before. With memories of happier times, I felt downcast for days and questioned what I was doing there. Surrounded by 70 people and a team of Christian staff, I felt utterly adrift and useless.

As the British camp director was still abroad and would not be arriving at camp for several more days, I decided to sit down and divulge the details of my divorce and the years of abuse I had suffered with another ministry staff person, an Albanian pastor whom I had known for five years through my previous interaction at the camp. "Pastor Erion" was a trusted friend, and while I feared becoming emotional while explaining my situation to him, I was able to get through a very succinct version of my story without my voice breaking.

Understandably, he was surprised and saddened – but not shocked. Pastor Erion had watched one of his own sisters suffer at the hands of a "Christian" man who actually beat her, and recognized that life does not always neatly follow biblical guidelines of repentance and reconciliation. He encouraged me not to despair. In Albania, as is the case in many countries, abuse of women is widespread – even within the Church. While he agreed in theory with my former pastor's assertion that "God can change anyone", Erion had seen far too much of the reality of abuse to be convinced that abusers usually repent. As do many pastors, Erion counsels couples in his village church. But ultimately, protection of women (and children) from all kinds of abuse when the situation does not change is a ministry of Christ that he seeks to fulfill. More than anyone else, this Balkan brother was relieved that I was now safe; healing; and regaining my confidence. He listened. He understood. He shared the Word of God with me. As conservative and "by-the-book" as this 30-something pastor is, not once did he use Scripture as a weapon against me. I went back to my tent that night feeling that a heavy burden I had carried across the Atlantic had been somewhat lifted.

The journey was only just beginning.

Far from treating me differently, or as a "second-class citizen," my friends and co-laborers for the Gospel encouraged me and showed nothing but compassion and understanding during those hard weeks. The relative seclusion of the beach camp and relaxed pace allowed me to spend time with God – alone. Those two weeks, I spent time with God – alone. Only He saw my tears. Walking down to the pier and watching the sun set over the Ionian Sea, I would just sit there. Sometimes I would read my Bible; sometimes just think. But always realizing I was in the presence of my Father; Who was my Defender and Protector. I knew that He had orchestrated everything perfectly, but I needed to experience it on an emotional level…which is hard to do, when you are running from your emotions.

One of the English lessons we taught the children at camp dealt with placing God's opinion above that of men. This was far too specific to be a coincidence. He seemed to be speaking directly to me, and there were mornings that I wanted to run from the discussion group I facilitated with a British team member. The basic truths about God's love we were teaching the children were long-forgotten promises I no longer really believed applied to me.

Taking us Across the World…to Get us to Listen?

It was here at camp that I could begin to move forward spiritually. As if to further assure me that He was there, I received a Facebook message from one of the young British staff women (who did not know me at all) the day after she left camp, asking if I was alright. She had sensed something was not right in my spirit, even though she was meeting me for the first time. After I shared a very abridged version of events with her, she responded:

> Marie,
>
> I cannot begin to imagine what you have been going through. I am thankful you have spoken to people at camp and pray they have been of great comfort and support for you. I appreciate your honesty and openness so much to share with me what's really been going on. God has a plan for bringing you to Albania this summer and I pray you will truly find some healing over the hardships of this year. I know God has good plans for you as he has promised to his people. It must be another load of hurt to have your pastor respond to you as he has. But as you can see from [names of ministry staff redacted] it is not the opinion held by all.

Above all it is God's thoughts we need to care about. And please remember that He loves you unconditionally! Draw close to Him and let His wings protect you during this tough time. And don't hurt yourself by not allowing yourself to rightfully have the emotions you are having. God knows above all how you are feeling. I just don't want you to think you need to hide it or feel you aren't getting involved in camp as you should. Because God may want this time in Albania to be where you can heal and be raw with all the feelings. I really pray I haven't spoken out of turn. And everything I have said makes sense. I will continue to pray for you and keep you in my thoughts. Your sister in Christ,

Lisa

Being Transparent – while Still Trusting God

The ministry leaders under whom I serve in Albania are good friends, but I had feared more rejection or subtle judgement once they knew of my divorce – justification notwithstanding. In fact, just the opposite happened. After explaining the situation to the Albanian pastor, I sat down with the camp director and later his wife – who had also seen such verbally-abusive situations in her own family. Not only was my decision supported, I was still embraced as the sister I'd always been. However, the lesson God taught me that week was that *it shouldn't matter*.

He affirms, loves and rejoices over me. The opinion of people (even *His* people) pales in significance. Even so, it was very freeing to be lifted up by friends who cared about me and understood, to sme degree, what I had been through.

We cannot live, as believers, in a vacuum. It is impossible to pretend that the opinions, acceptance, love or approval of others – particularly of fellow Christians – do not matter. We were created to live in fellowship, and God grieves when His children alienate one another. And yet sometimes, in order to break the walls of others-induced shame that have kept us from Him, He needs to isolate us to where we can't run away anymore. And when we finally start listening to His voice of truth, He may confirm His love to us through other people. Until we discover that His is the only voice that truly matters, however, we may stay stuck listening to the sound of our own confusion, doubt, and condemnation of those claiming to speak on His behalf.

I expected to be used to help others understand God's Word that summer. Instead, God ministered His grace and healing to me – in a remote coastal campsite; without friends to fall back on; half a world away.

The Aftershock

Mere weeks after I returned to the United States in September 2016, the emails demanding more "meetings" started up again. Although God had comforted and reassured me that I was His, the escalation of my former church's "discipline proceedings" against me (which I described in chapters 8-9) again threatened to destroy my peace. Exhausted by the 50-hour weeks I was working in order to survive, and worn down by the pastor's constant gaslighting, I was on the verge of a nervous breakdown.

Without his knowing the details of my situation, my new pastor emailed me one morning simply to ask how I was (no one at my former church had ever done that). Alarmed by my answer, he and his wife arranged to meet me at Panera Bread that very afternoon...where he let me cry and shared the Gospel with me for three straight hours. Two women in the church, around my mother's age, subsequently "adopted" me. They would often invite me to their homes for coffee in weeks following. At Christmas, I learned that someone had anonymously donated a "love offering" so that I could buy my children Christmas gifts.

It was the most heartbreaking period of my life, but throughout the whole ordeal I was surrounded by strong, Christian friends who lifted me up at my lowest points. They didn't simply quote Scripture verses to me and assume that was enough; they sustained my life. Yet the dichotomy was striking in how one church's leadership took the stance that I was the one in sin, simply for standing up for myself; whilst another church emulated Christ's role as a Protector and Defender of the innocent. In His mercy, Christ has provided true shepherds – like my current pastor – who continuously reveal Him to the hurting. Relentlessly, he takes me back to Scripture to show me how we are all a part of "His Story" and partakers of His grace.

Spiritual abuse can be the most damaging type of all, because it skews the victim's view of God. If an institution claiming to act in His Name is systematically tormenting the weakest and most vulnerable members of His Body, the sheep will be so beaten down that eventually they will leave. It would have been impossible to hold onto my faith in God if I had not been embraced by His children, including fellow "broken toys." What bystanders may not realize, however, is the enormous mental, emotional and even physical toll "standing one's ground" takes on an abuse survivor.

Medical Professionals as Allies

Sometimes the trauma, fear and/or depression caused by abuse becomes so intense that basic daily functioning is difficult. This is especially true for a woman after she has left the abusive relationship. The abuser, seeking revenge for the loss of control (or pride) she has caused him will increase his intimidation attempts and gaslighting as much as circumstance allows. In my case, it was not the memories of abuse in my marriage that caused my physical symptoms, but rather the psychological pressure to "reconcile" and the calculated harassment from the senior pastor that caused my anxiety attacks. This secondary spiritual abuse pushed me to the edge of a mental breakdown. (Both Stephanie and the hospital chaplain were ready to testify to this if I had brought a civil suit against the church.)

Regardless of the source or type of abuse, women who have been through this trauma very often experience physical symptoms of depression and anxiety which make it difficult to function in day-to-day life. Severe insomnia, debilitating depression, fear bordering on paranoia, frequent headaches and an inability to concentrate are common mental effects of long-term abuse. Survivors of emotional abuse often struggle with complex post-traumatic stress disorder (PTSD), muscular pain, vascular problems, brain fog, weight loss, sleep disorders, and more.

While medication may not always be the answer, there are times when the symptoms must be treated with anti-depressant or anti-anxiety medications so that the woman will be able to subsequently deal with the emotional and spiritual effects of the abuse. Anti-anxiety medications, such as Xanax, Klonopin, Valium and Ativan are strong and can be habit-forming. For this reason, physicians tend to prefer *not* to prescribe them to patients unless the panic attacks are so severe that there are no other options. More commonly, a low dose of an anti-depressant (Selective Serotonin Reuptake Inhibitor, or SSRI) will be prescribed to treat symptoms of both anxiety and depression.

The Breaking Point

The effects of anxiety and emotional trauma are cumulative over time. After my first panic attack at the hospital, I agreed to see a domestic abuse counselor for three visits through an employee assistance program – hoping, as the chaplain did, that she would at least be able to persuade my former pastor to halt his pressure on me for the sake of my mental and physical health. Although the counselor did not pressure me to take anti-anxiety or depression medication, she mentioned it as an option – one which I quickly declined.

As a trained nouthetic counselor, I was taught to view the mental health field with suspicion. We are told that taking anti-depressants is the equivalent of using a hammer to smash the warning light on a dashboard, rather than looking under the hood to diagnose the problem. We are also told that physicians want to push psychotropic medications on patients, in order to keep them dependent and increase revenue for the pharmacological industry. "Looking under the hood" to a nouthetic counselor generally means identifying some personal sin that is responsible for the individual's anxiety or depression. (There certainly was sin causing my mental anguish – that of my then-pastor's.) Blackmail, especially by a supposed "man of God", can wreak havoc on a woman's emotional health, especially when she is still trying to process the abuse she experienced by her partner. When I first heard the term "panic attack", I assumed it was a psychosomatic thing that could be overcome with correct thinking. In fact, it is the body's neurological response to the adrenal system going into overdrive – the nervous system simply doesn't know what to do with the additional stress, and goes into an adrenalin-driven fight-or-flight mode.

My primary care physician, who is much younger than me, was aware of the situation and was most concerned about my inability to sleep, concentrate at work, and suicidal thoughts. He put me on a low dose of Lexapro and Trazadone, two anti-depressants (the latter of which treats insomnia), simply in order to address my physical symptoms so that I could function normally again. We discussed other ways of handling the anxiety, and I shared that I had begun going to the gym; had taken legal action to fight my ex-husband's contempt of court order; and had added a pet kitten to our family. He was also very supportive of my meeting with my new pastor and processing things as they happened without being swallowed in despair. "These things like standing up for yourself and having a strong support system in place are going to help you far more than any pill I could give you," he said. Nevertheless, the 50 mg. dose of Trazadone once again allowed me to get a few hours of sleep per night, and my heart rate returned to normal. After just a few months, I was back on track enough to keep moving forward without any medication at all – another important victory won.

The Importance of Church Fellowship

Even if I had not been bullied out, I would not have been able to heal from the pain inflicted if I had stayed at my former church. Having my ex-husband glowering at me from several seats away; the strain of "keeping up appearances" as a happy family; and knowing my decision to divorce on grounds of abuse did not fit their theological paradigm combined to make leaving inevitable. Although I had the benefit of strong hermeneutical training and was well aware I had ample grounds for divorce, those in "authority" claiming to speak *ex cathedra* had loud, damning voices.

Once I found the courage to return to church, my relationship with God once again became the anchor for my life. A friend of mine, who had been very supportive throughout all of my dealings with my former church, had herself been excommunicated by the elders there about ten years earlier for the same reason. Although she had been in physical danger, the leaders at the time had been unyielding and she consequently also experienced a horribly painful and confusing season. One of the strongest and most joyful Christians I know, "Brenda" invited me to her church and introduced me to the pastor (whom I had known only by sight).

Over the course of the next few months, as I sorted through the painful emotions of strained relationships with my children (as they still attended my former church, it was hard for them to see their mother being harassed) and struggled to keep my faith in God. It was my new pastor, David, along with his wife Jennifer, who sat down with me for hours at a time and looked at the Bible. Far from just throwing verses at me, we discussed scriptural topics and how they applied to my life at great length. Re-affirming my identity in Christ was the starting point if I was ever able to heal, and he expressed far more concern about what was going on within me than the storm I was caught in on the outside. As one Christian counselor put it, "After an earthquake, there are always aftershocks. You, right now, are in the aftershock."

A Place of Refuge

Desperate to survive the storm (and preserve my sanity), I reached out to Pastor David. He had said from the beginning that he wanted to provide a place of refuge for me, and for his church to be a place of healing. I am not the sort of person to make enemies, and to be so despised by a member of the clergy – for no other reason than I defied him and stood up for myself – was jarring. Although I knew very well that these men did not speak for God (and that I was obeying him), being pursued, accused and ultimately threatened with slander to the congregation I so loved was a surreal experience. Somewhat like being in the "in group" in middle school cliques, an adolescent or teen may one day find him or herself "on the outs" – rejected by the group, for some arbitrary reason.

However, God is not fickle like humans are and does not turn His back on His children because they do not "play by the rules" others have invented. It can be very difficult for anyone experiencing spiritual abuse or ostracism to differentiate between *religion* and *God*. "God" becomes, in the victim's consciousness, a distant and unapproachable impersonal force; rather than the loving and ever-faithful Father Scripture portrays Him to be. Pastor David understood this crisis, and arranged for me to meet with an experienced counselor from his congregation. Karen, a wise and compassionate woman, had been in marriage counseling ministry for 25 years at that point. More importantly, she cared about me deeply and treated me like a daughter. At my new church, I never felt that I had to hide my tears from anyone. On my worst day, I could feel like I belonged there. I have often looked back and thought, if I hadn't been rescued by these true believers who really demonstrated the love of Christ, the spiritual bullying I endured might have caused me to walk away from God altogether.

Abuse survivor Jen Grice candidly admits that the pain one goes through during an upheaval of life is not something that time alone will heal. A deeper trust in God, and His purposes for us, is mandatory if we are ever to move forward. On her blog, a source of encouragement for abused and/or divorced Christian women, she writes about the antidote to anxiety:

> What I had no idea at the time was that God was building my case. I couldn't see into the future to know that it would all be worked out, that I would be taken care of, and I would be protected from further harm, so I battled with fear and anxiety as I worried about the future. All I could do was to hold tightly to God's promises, knowing that God knew my character, my heart for integrity, and my reverence for Him.

> In the end, God does work everything out. And we can conquer our fears and anxiety with courage and strength knowing that no matter how bad it looks now, or even how much worse it gets, that God is on our side building our case and preparing the way.

> Hope is knowing something good can and will come out of something bad.[46]

In the next chapter, we will explore more deeply some of the truths about Who God is and how He sees us. Abuse survivors desperately need to embrace the promises God has given in His Word in order to begin healing and moving forward towards new life.

---

[46] http://jengrice.com/blog/conquering-fear-and-anxiety-after-divorce.html

CHAPTER 11

Abuse Survivors: Re-Claim Your Identity in Christ

"I have loved you with an everlasting love." – God

Once the dust of removing herself from an abusive situation settles, a Christian woman still needs to deal with the emotional and spiritual fallout of what has been done to her – whether at the hands of her husband, her church, or both. Bewilderment, feelings of betrayal, abandonment by trusted friends, and even feeling forsaken by God Himself are common experiences for a woman who has endured domestic abuse of any kind.

Taught to see her husband as her "covering" and to submit to him as unto the Lord, the line between how her husband views her and how she believes God views her becomes blurred. If her husband sees her as incompetent and treats her with contempt, unconsciously she comes to believe God is disappointed in her and views her contemptuously as well. Her very view of God has become skewed, and it becomes difficult for an abused woman to relate to Him. Add to this shame-conditioning the additional betrayal of spiritual abuse and victim-blaming by her church, and a woman can be made to feel very far away from God.

She must re-learn the truth God has promised her in His Word: "The LORD is close to the brokenhearted and saves those who are crushed in spirit" (Psalm 34:18). There are few people on earth more "crushed in spirit" than women who have endured abusive marriages. This is why it is so crucial that she not only stay connected to a church where the truth and hope of the Gospel (the Person and work of Jesus Christ on her behalf) is proclaimed, but that she has help in rejecting the lies she has internalized.

Stages of Healing

Christian and secular counselors alike have identified stages in the grief and healing process. With some variance, abuse survivors must walk through their own version of these "stages" in order to again become healthy, functioning individuals no longer suffering from the trauma of the past. There are many excellent books that cover each part of the recovery process in great detail, and I would highly recommend any abuse survivor read and apply the principles laid out in them (see "Recommended Resources" at the end of this book for suggestions). However, in order to understand the progression of overcoming a traumatic past, a brief overview of the usual healing process at this point would be helpful. Processing grief and overcoming fear takes time, and an abuse survivor need not rush the process. There are bound to be steps forward and backward as she encounters new obstacles and hostility, but with a strong support system and consciousness of who she is in Christ, there is great hope of healing.

Usually, a woman is in denial for years that what she is experiencing really is abuse, and the first step will be recognition and acceptance that she is in a destructive situation. She must change her circumstances, even if no one else will help (or even believe) her. Writer Natalie Herbranson describes this "waking up" stage as feeling like jumping into an icy cold lake at the beginning of spring, just after the ice has thawed. It is a terrifying realization. Learning as much as she can (through the testimonies of others and studying the issue of abuse) will help her realize that what has happened to her is not uncommon, nor is it her fault. Learning how God views mistreatment and reviling of His children is crucially important to avoid the guilt that she will surely face. It is also vital that she receive godly counsel from mature Christians as she learns to discern God's will for her future.

Accepting what Happened

The first step in moving towards a healthier relationship with God for one thus traumatized is to accept that while God did not *cause* the sin against her, He *allowed* it in her life. While He promises to "work all things together for the good of those who love Him" (Romans 8:28), Scripture tells us that He has taken notice of all her tears (Psalm 56:8) and will wipe them away one day (Revelation 21:4). He punishes the oppressor, and vindicates the innocent (Psalm 37:6; Isaiah 54:17). He was present in her suffering, not as an impersonal bystander but as a deeply invested Father. While her emotions may be telling her differently, He has never abandoned her in her trial. In this knowledge, she may accept that her situation is not beyond His notice or redemption. While there will still be days when she asks "Why? Where was God? Why did this happen to me?," her faith will stand on the firm knowledge that He was there; He cares for her; and if she follows Him, as He did with Joseph when his brothers sold him into slavery, God will bring good out of tragedy.

Grieving is an ongoing stage that lessens over time, but may never fully go away. We will discuss the effects of depression that often occur at this stage a little later in the chapter, but for now it's important to acknowledge that the grieving stage is inevitable when a woman faces the truth of what she has endured. As painful as the mistreatment in the relationship was, it had come to seem "normal." Change is frightening, and a huge hole is left in her heart. In order to begin to heal, she must move through the grief cycle.

Stages of the Grief Cycle

"NORMAL" FUNCTIONING

RETURN TO MEANINGFUL LIFE

Shock and Denial
- Avoidance
- Confusion
- Fear
- Numbness
- Blame

Anger
- Frustration
- Anxiety
- Irritation
- Embarrassment
- Shame

- Empowerment
- Security
- Self-esteem
- Meaning

Acceptance
- Exploring options
- A new plan in place

Dialogue and Bargaining
- Reaching out to others
- Desire to tell one's story
- Struggle to find meaning for what has happened

Depression and Detachment
- Overwhelmed
- Blahs
- Lack of energy
- Helplessness

As the abuse survivor learns new and healthy boundaries, she eventually will emerge out of the grieving stage and into the new life God has for her. This involves work – accepting new (and old) responsibilities; taking ownership of her own decisions; continuing involvement in Bible studies and fellowship groups; defining her priorities and goals – and pursuing them. Some women make the mistake of becoming overly-busy and involved, thinking that additional work, goals and projects will provide a distraction and new sense of purpose in their lives. This can actually lead to burnout – her spiritual well-being at this point is still fragile, and time alone with God (as well as rest) is still the most important source of her healing. While she is re-building her life, at this point the abusive ex-spouse may make life particularly difficult for her. "Abusive individuals do not want you to have healthy boundaries, and they will do everything in their power to maintain control," says Klejwa. Smear campaigns usually work in the man's favor, but regardless, a woman need keep her resolve, keep her eyes fixed on Jesus, and keep working towards freedom and wholeness.

Dealing with the fallout of spiritual abuse, broken friendships, strained relationships with children, and crises of faith is the ripple-effect of standing up to abuse. Now that she is stronger, the woman needs to figure out where the flaws in her thinking lay that had led to her faith being shaken. For example, believing the lie that there is redemptive value in suffering inflicted by another's sin is common patriarchal conditioning. It may take years to completely reject this premise and "renew her mind" in this regard. She must rely on the Scriptures time and again to see how closely God treasures His daughters, and to realize there is no allowance for oppression or abuse.

Rest and time to rebuild relationships (and develop new ones) is all part of the process. Finally, walking in grace and truth, she reaches the point where all the remnants of the past remain in the past. Confidently moving ahead in her faith, her career, and her relationships, she is now better equipped to help others who are struggling under the weight of abuse. She can be a voice of wisdom to those under the bondage of teachers who claim that abuse isn't real; it isn't serious; and if it does exist, it must have been her fault. Now that she has turned back, she can help her sisters.

Setting Healthy Boundaries

A woman coming out of an abusive relationship, first and foremost, needs to ensure her physical safety (and that of her children, when applicable). Having an escape plan in cases where her partner may get violent unpredictably is important – women's shelters recommend having a bag packed with clothes, emergency cash, and other immediate necessities at all times. She should get in the habit of backing her car into the driveway to enable a swifter escape, if necessary. Keeping the phone number on hand of a domestic abuse hotline and those of several friends and/or relatives who could take her in temporarily is also advisable. Once she is out of the house, she should file a police report as soon as possible – this will help her greatly in obtaining a restraining order, should she need to go to probate court.

In cases of physical abuse, it is absolutely imperative to involve the local authorities – men who beat their wives are volatile and not to be trusted, no matter how many promises they may make in order to lure their victims back home. Be aware that many churches will attempt to use 1 Corinthians 6:1-11 (admonishment about lawsuits among believers) to castigate an abuse victim for involving law enforcement, but the church has neither the expertise nor authority to ensure the woman's safety. As we have seen in earlier chapters, the Church is subject to the secular authorities, and God has made provision for the protection of women even in the Levitical Law. If a man in the United States hits his neighbor's wife, he will go to jail. Why should he get a pass for hitting his own wife?

In cases of non-physical abuse, which can be just as harmful, the same principal of setting boundaries still applies. While her physical safety may not be endangered, her emotional and mental health can be badly jeopardized by continued contact with her abuser and his allies. This is especially true when the abuser manages to enlist the church leadership to support him, and the woman is dealing with secondary harassment.

When Karen Hinkley (see footnote in chapter 9) was "pursued" and re-victimized by Matt Chandler and his team of elders at The Village Church in Texas, she ultimately packed up and left town – moving all the way across the country to start her life over again. Even though she eventually won, and the church leaders flew out to her new home in North Carolina to apologize (and beg her not to move forward with a lawsuit), her life was destroyed. She has since completed a law degree and begun her life anew, but the chaos and slander against her in her home church and community made physical distance necessary. When my story of similar "pursuit" by my former church was covered by the media, the backlash against me was also considerable. I fully expected to walk outside one morning and find my tires slashed. As I share joint custody of my children with my former husband, and my interpreting career is based in the Boston area, moving away wasn't really an option for me. But with my pastor's help, I learned to eliminate the negative voices in my life as much as possible – and trust Christ to vindicate me where ignoring them was not possible.

One example of a healthy boundary I set was realizing I do not have to respond to every message sent to me – whether pseudo-friendly notes fishing for information, or "setting me up" for admonishment. For an abuse survivor, realizing she is not accountable to bystanders with incomplete knowledge and no direct involvement in her situation is very freeing. Setting boundaries helps keep her mind clear and negates distractions, so she may focus on the important business of caring for herself and her children. There are times when going completely "no contact" with her abuser may be necessary in separation, especially when dealing with an individual with extreme narcissistic tendencies. Other times, civility but distance may be more appropriate – especially when the communication is not threatening, constant, or there are children involved.

Document Everything

Controlling men will never give up – sarcastic or belligerent calls and emails, violation of court orders, and frightening confrontations in an attempt to intimidate their former victims are commonplace. A woman should keep records of all these incidents, with dates and as many specific details as possible. Testimony from others (including the children) if he is attempting to destroy her reputation should also be documented. If it is necessary to have any contact with him, the woman should always bring a friend as a witness. Save and document all written communication, especially when it can be used to prove violation of court orders (in cases of separation or divorce). Whether separated or still together, documenting all incidents of abuse *in writing* is crucial for the pastor if he is attempting to counsel. If he ignores or fails to act on it, it may be valuable evidence if the case escalates to the court system.

Guarding Against Bitterness

One of the common accusations brought against abuse survivors who speak out (especially those who have endured spiritual abuse) is that they are "bitter." Exposing wickedness is not "bitterness"; it indicates a healthy moral compass. A woman who stands up and says "No more. I will no longer be threatened, intimidated, bullied, humiliated etc." is not necessarily "bitter." Usually, such a woman is more like Abigail who, in 1 Samuel 25:1-42, courageously undermined her wicked husband (instead of submitting to him) and thereby saved her family and people. Was she rebuked by God? No; she was *blessed*. God never intended for women to submit to an abusive husband and remain in an unhealthy, destructive (or sometimes dangerous) relationship. Yet taking action to protect herself, and especially speaking about the abuse, will often invite the charge of "bitterness". It seems to be a word wielded as a generic conversation-stopper in evangelical churches, some of which find the exposure of domestic abuse far too inconvenient a truth to countenance.

On the flip side, however, is the very real possibility that an abuse survivor can turn inward and nurse self-pity, especially if she is lacking in support or ongoing godly counsel. While understandable, self-pity and unforgiveness coupled with anger can lead into a downward spiral towards bitterness. However, while survivors of mistreatment have often been labeled by their churches as "bitter" for standing up to the abuse (citing Hebrews 12:15), the true "root of bitterness" mentioned in the context of the passage isn't an attitude. The "bitter root" is a person, like Esau, whose anger and hatred poisoned everyone around him. The apostle is telling the church to watch out for profane and worldly people who poison everyone else. As we have seen in an earlier chapter, this includes the contentious; the revilers. The abusive man fits that category perfectly. It is the abusive individual(s) who are the "bitter roots" corrupting the congregation – not their victims.

Nevertheless, bitterness itself grows where unresolved anger and hurt meet. Nursing and rehashing old wounds will eat away at a person's soul, affecting her mood and relationships with other people if it is not dealt with biblically. The past only exists if you continue to live there. We can't go back and change the past, so whatever has been, accept that God has allowed it and will not allow it to destroy you.

Refocusing on the One Whose Opinion Matters

As bewildering as the aftermath of my divorce was, what helped me avoid the trap of bitterness was the wise counsel of my pastor, David, who would sit down with me regularly. In a statement to the media, he explained his agenda as "not to comment on the theology or practices of other local churches, but to be a refuge and a place of healing for Marie." He cared about how I was doing spiritually above all, and taught me to accept the apology I would never receive.

"There is something within all of us that deeply desires to be vindicated, to have others see and acknowledge that we are right," he said. As a pastor who also works as a professional soccer coach, David is no stranger to criticism and character attacks. But the secret to rising above such derision is in recognizing that we are never going to change the minds of those who have already sided against us, and learning to rest in God's opinion of us – not people's. This is what will produce the true peace that surpasses understanding, and allows us to rest in the Father's arms during the midst of the storm.

"Those who know you know that you did the right thing; those who want desperately to believe their pastor's version will believe it anyway, no matter how much evidence you produce in your own defense. If anyone understands what you're going through, it is Jesus, he reminded me. 'Jesus was falsely accused and called a devil. His followers were excommunicated by the Pharisees – just like they're trying to do to you. Yet He never defended Himself. He didn't need to; He had His Father's approval.'"

As noted in the last chapter, the approval of other people shouldn't matter. We know this; we pay lip-service to it. Yet it is incredibly difficult for anyone who has been maligned to walk in this truth and not let gossip and outright lies affect her. Prayer becomes even more important for the abuse survivor to intentionally re-connect with her Heavenly Father on a daily basis. Otherwise, new attacks – whether gaslighting from her abuser, chastisement, or slander – will send her into a new tailspin.

Remembering that God Loves Her

After being abused by someone she trusted, learning to rest in the assurance of God's personal love for her is an extremely difficult, but vitally important, part of healing for a woman. While related to the previous point about being concerned with how God views her (rather than the opinions of others), believing again that she is *loved* is a deeper heart issue. One may evaluate her choices and actions as being necessary and without sin (and therefore consider herself "right with God"), but truly believing she is loved by Him when she has been reviled by her husband (and possibly others) is a much harder matter.

In our first meeting together, after I had been attending his church for several months, David noted that I never took Communion on Sundays. I admitted that he was right, and he challenged me to consider why I hadn't. While I couldn't identify any particular sin in my life, it was a general sense of "dirtiness" I carried from the ordeal at the previous church that made me feel unworthy to be in *any* church, anywhere. I had stayed close to God throughout both the 20 years of pain in my marriage and the post-divorce ordeal, but it still seemed too fresh to take Communion in a corporate worship setting.

He then put his finger on a truth so deep I had not yet acknowledged it myself: "Deep down, you fear that God doesn't love you anymore." He was right. I had no response. He didn't need to open the Bible to remind me of the lavish grace God pours out on the Prodigal Son; the woman caught in adultery; the thief on the cross. The stories are so many and so familiar that they lose their personal impact in a moment of deep crisis. The age-old fear "Does God *really* love me?" whispers in the dark that we are unworthy, unloved by others, and presumably unlovable. We project this onto God, even without realizing it.

Divine Orchestration and Messages

Doubting God's love is not a rational misunderstanding which can be remedied with a verse or two memorized. We can be told repeatedly that "God loves you," but it takes time and a deliberate decision to trust in this truth again in order for it to take root in an abuse survivor's soul. Connecting with a supportive fellowship of believers is important, as isolation leads to loneliness and more doubt. However, knowing God's personal love and tender care is still a solitary journey. It hinges on the individual's relationship with her Heavenly Father and willingness to listen to Him.

Several months after I began counseling with my pastor, friends of mine from another church invited me to attend a two-day women's retreat with them. I looked forward to spending time with my friends, but was not really expecting much spiritually. It was a rather intimate gathering of approximately two dozen women, and the first evening the speaker – a very low-key and gentle woman who had an incredibly strong relationship with God – told us that His message for each of us that weekend was to know how passionately He loved each one of us and desired us to joyfully use our gifts. She neither knew me nor knew I was not a part of that church group, but looking straight at me she said, "Some of you don't feel like you belong here. You've been rejected at times, and are unsure of Father's love. You're not even certain He can use you. I'm here to tell you that's not true."

Later during the retreat, she and others were praying together over me and without knowing the details of my circumstances, gave me the following word of knowledge: "God loves you. Trust God. He is going to bring good out of all the negative things in your life." The following Sunday, a quote in my own pastor's sermon confirmed this word: *"Your identity is in Me. You are My beloved. All of these other identities, all of these other judgements are not the real story of you! The real story of you is: 'Nothing at all will stop My love for you, nothing; and in Me, there is no, absolutely no, condemnation.'"* I was unable to find the source of the quote, but it is very much in line with Romans 8:31-39 and Romans 8:1, which declare that nothing in all of creation can separate us from the love of God and there is no condemnation for those who are in Christ.

Although this was simple Scriptural truth, the timing and means in which God spoke it to me was highly personal. I believe that as any woman (or man) broken by the hurt and shame of abuse earnestly seeks a revelation of His individual love, He will faithfully reveal His heart to her in an equally personal way.

Jesus: The Antidote to Shame

In a meditation on the toxic effect of spiritual abuse, Fount Lee Shults writes:

> Shame makes us feel like we don't belong, like we have no right to be here. We feel illegitimate. This is how religious groups sometimes control their people. The shame of the leaders makes them feel illegitimate as leaders if they are not able to keep their people in line. So they use the threat of shunning to control the outward behavior of their group. This strategy is used by political powers, educational and business institutions as well as churches. The threat of being fired (shunned) can cause people to keep silent when they should speak up.[47]

As my pastor reminded me, it was the religious people – notably the Pharisees – who condemned Jesus and tried to "shun" Him by undermining His ministry. Ultimately, the crucifixion was the highest form of shame, which He endured to carry all of *our* sin and shame. We no longer live under condemnation, but modern-day Pharisees use a similar (if more subtle) tactic. How can authoritarian church leaders control (by shunning) people using pornography; having secret affairs; cheating on their income taxes; or any number of other "clandestine" sins? Furthermore, the reason it is the woman they will most commonly shame is because the very structure of patriarchal authoritarianism automatically puts women in a defenseless position. The deck is stacked against a woman in these types of churches, so that if she does speak out the natural reaction will be to try to silence her. If she refuses to subject herself to more abuse, she will be shamed. The "wayward sheep" is now the victim, painted forever in the congregation's eyes with a "scarlet letter."

Jesus puts no such letter on her.

In a 2012 national conference on guilt and shame, CCEF counselor Winston Smith said,

> When we witness a divorce, we often focus on the headlines: what went wrong, who is responsible, custody arrangements, financial needs, and sometimes even church discipline. It's easy to miss the insidious work that guilt and shame are doing behind the scenes. Divorced spouses feel like "damaged goods" and "second-class citizens" in the church. Children blame themselves, and well-meaning helpers litter the path with half-

---

[47] Shults, Fount Lee. On Word Ministries, online devotional.

truths and pat answers. Guilt and shame are often complicated or masked by silence, anxiety, anger, and bitterness.[48]

Even if divorce never enters the picture, the abuse victim carries an irrational sense of shame. She believes something is fundamentally wrong with her; broken beyond repair. She wants desperately to believe that she did not deserve the mistreatment, but her abuser – more powerful than her – will always insinuate otherwise. Shame, unlike guilt, is not necessarily linked to a specific action or wrongdoing. It is a more generalized sense that there is something inherently wrong with us. Nouthetic counselors often fail in their attempts to help depressed persons, victims of abuse (particularly sexual abuse), and others struggling with shame because they seek an easily-identifiable 'sin-label' to identify the source of the person's shame. It is rarely, if ever, that simple. When we return to the Gospel, we see a Savior Who goes out of His way to meet people suffering in the shadows from shame – lepers; adulterers; tax collectors; a five-times divorced Samaritan woman ostracized by her community; even the Apostle Peter who denied knowing Him.

The poison of shame is one that Christ came to remove and replace with joy and abundant life (John 10:10). It dissipates in His presence, whether the source is religious leaders or one's own past life which the believer is convinced she can never move past. To the one shamed and wounded by the sin of another, He says "Come to Me, and I will give you rest" (Matthew 11:28).

Putting it Together

Learning to believe, receive and abide in the unconditional, personal, Father-love of God and know in the marrow of her bones that Christ has removed all shame from her is the obstacle any abuse survivor must overcome in order to move forward in her relationship with Him. God does not see her as "damaged goods" because of the hateful words cast at her or degrading actions done to her; nor is she "a sheep who has strayed from the fold" if she has stood up to the abuser(s). He sees her as a beloved daughter; a cherished member of His Body with unique gifts and characteristics. He has already removed any shame she may feel, so that she may draw near boldly to Him (Hebrews 4:16) and will not change His opinion of her based upon how she may feel on any given day.

For someone deprived of love and affection for so long, these truths seem

---

[48] Winston Smith, *Guilt and Shame* (CCEF National Conference 2012), "Shame in Divorce"

so good as to hardly be true! But this is the very reason she needs to run *to* and not *away* from God in abusive (and post-abusive) situations. Without regular time renewing her mind in the Word and being encouraged by other believers, despair may overtake her when the storm never seems to pass.

As I type these words, it is Father's Day 2017. I am thinking of a book that helped me understand the Father-love of God recently and was instrumental in my own healing, *He Loves Me!* by Wayne Jacobsen. He contrasts the image of a "mean God" many believers hold with the God of Scripture, Who seeks out the lost; brings to repentance with loving kindness; and loves with an everlasting love wholly independent of His children's behavior on any given day. He describes how, forgetting we are His eternal children, Christians often have the tendency to "live less loved"- thinking and acting as if God loves them less in certain circumstances than at times when they are "performing" well. This is not how even earthly fathers view their children, and it is antithetical to the Gospel.

The antidote to abuse-induced shame is a deep knowledge of how much one is loved and treasured by the King of Kings. Once you know that love, you cannot help but be changed by it.

The Ability to Forgive One's Abuser

Forgiveness, it is often said, is "a gift you give yourself". It may well be that, as it is a necessary part of healing from abuse and maturing spiritually, but it is also obedience to God (Matthew 6:14; Mark 11:26). Here, however, we must be careful to consider what forgiveness is (and isn't), as in cases of abuse spiritual advisors sometimes rush the victim to "forgive and forget" too quickly while her abuser remains in sin.

Forgiveness is not:

- Pretending the abuse never happened;
- Reconciling with the abuser, absent evidence of a complete heart-change;
- Putting one's self (or children) in danger (particularly relevant in cases where physical and/or sexual assault has been documented);
- Covering up the abuser's sin or justifying it in the name of "righteous suffering".

Forgiveness is:

- Accepting that no apology will be forthcoming, and being at peace with it;

- A willingness to let go of revenge (a desire to "get even");
- A desire to see the abuser repent and be restored;
- A commitment to live at peace (so far as it depends on her) with the abuser and his allies, without sacrificing her safety or emotional well-being in the process.

Forgiveness is an important component of an abuse survivor's healing, because without being willing to "let [him] go" in her heart, and accept that God allowed the trauma, she will be much more prone to bitterness. Re-playing and stewing over what kind of a person could and would inflict such pain on her will not help her move forward, or grow in Christ. It will also cause her to put up relational walls with other people she feels may hurt her, and thus thwart healthy relationships in the future.

In some cases, an abuser is simply so deceived in his heart that he actually believes what he is doing is in obedience to God. Recently, there was yet another case in the news of a strict evangelical couple convicted for beating one of their children to death, and critically injuring one of their other adopted children. They had been using David and Debi Pearl's infamous book *To Train Up a Child* as a guide for administering corporal punishment, and when interviewed, the Pearls defended their abusive teachings on the grounds that "he who spares the rod hates his child" (Proverbs 13:24). In a less extreme way, some Christian men within patriarchal churches actually believe that controlling their wives like children and reviling them with verbal attacks is part of what it means to be the "spiritual leader" in their household. Unless this is corrected scripturally, in a wide-spread teaching of what it means to "love, honor and cherish" their wives as equals, certain proof texts will always be used to justify spousal abuse. Like Saul and those killing the early Christians, such men truly are convinced that they are in service to God.

Fortunately, not all (or even the majority) of Christian men believe or behave this way. For a long time following my experience, I was afraid of men – Christian men in particular. Pastor David explained and demonstrated to me the power of forgiveness, seeking to be like Christ as He prayed, "Father forgive them; they know not what they do" (Luke 23:34). There are many times when those operating from a pharisaical-like understanding of religion will simply not see how their actions, attitudes and teachings about women and the marriage relationship run counter to the Gospel.

Other times, the abuse is deliberate and pre-calculated. Controlling and abusive men generally are sane and know exactly what they are doing, as they seem able to turn it on and off when necessary (i.e. to protect their "good Christian" image in front of other people). This is one reason the testimony of abused wives is hard to believe by some in the church – the abuser can so easily portray himself as a bastion of society; a wonderful husband; even "father of the year." No one sees what goes on behind closed doors. The woman knows she has been a marked target, and she knows her abuser's tactics for hurting her. He has studied her weak points, and will take full advantage to exploit them to the greatest extent possible. This kind of calculated cruelty is *extremely* hard to forgive, but the survivor needs to rely on her support system to insulate herself and relinquish her "right" to get even if she desires to ever be free of him.

This does not mean, as so many churches teach, that she should be rushed into a contrived "reconciliation process" with the man who has thus sought to destroy her. Abuse is an attack on another individual made in the very image of God, and needs to be taken seriously for the pathological problem that it is. Can she forgive in her heart, giving up her "rights" to vengeance, and commit her abuser to God for judgment? Yes. Should she go back to him, and subject herself to continued torment? A categorical no.

Finally, how can local churches help end the problem of marital abuse, which so often rises up in their midst when there is an inbred system of inequality? How can we maintain a complementarian belief system, without relegating half the congregation to second-class status (and thereby setting them up for abuse)? In our final chapter, we will consider these questions.

CHAPTER 12

Towards a Healthier Complementarian Model

*"And I'm not anti-marriage, nor am I anti-men.
I'm anti-abuse, anti-control, anti-oppression. I know
now that once a marriage turns abusive, it's no longer a
marriage, no longer binding, no longer safe."*
*– Anonymous abuser survivor and blogger who
goes by pseudonym "Fixing Her Eyes"*[49]

With all previously said about:

- The existence of abuse in the Church;
- How some churches perpetuate the cycle (and add secondary spiritual abuse on top);
- While other churches embrace hurting women and help them find hope and healing in Christ;

We need to ask:

- What are some ways the universal Church can stop tolerating the cycle of abuse so common in complementarian congregations?
- How can the Body of Christ collectively become part of the solution to end abuse, in all its myriad forms?

These are difficult questions and the answers are complex. The process begins with recognizing the problem and the immense harm emotional abuse does to Christian women, especially when done in the Name of Christ. We have laid out some of the extra-biblical teaching and how it conditions women's thinking; heaps false guilt on them for their husbands' failings; and sets them

---

[49] http://www.fixinghereyes.org/single-post/2017/05/09/I-didnt-leave-my-husband

up both for a feverish attempt at their interpretation of "perfection" and to accept abuse as "God's will". To abandon such teaching is not to plunge the Church into liberalism; rather, it is to return it to the pure teaching of Jesus, who never demeaned or discredited women. The Gospel, as we have seen, is "Good News" for women as well as men, and it is not necessary to abandon Scripture's teaching on men and women's equality (but difference in roles) in order to combat abuse.

The egalitarians within the Church have traditionally done a better job at exposing oppression of women and giving them a voice to speak than the complementarian side. However, it is my conviction that even under male headship of the Church, this deep-rooted problem can be brought to light and combatted with the power of the Gospel. The Bible itself is full of references to God's protection of the innocent and provision for the oppressed, the widow, and the orphan – in today's day, we must extend this to include the abused women (and sometimes children) who have had to flee abusive (although churchgoing) men. Rather than embrace them, far too many complementarian churches have marginalized such victims and even stigmatized these women with three words from one verse wrenched out of context: *"God hates divorce."*

Yes. And He hates abuse even more.

Believe Them

The words "I believe you" are incredibly empowering to an abused woman, who perhaps for many years has been told the problem is "all in her head" or she "is crazy" by her husband. She may even question her own sanity at times. A victim of gaslighting and other abusive tactics in her marriage wrote anonymously:

> I was stunned to realize something a couple of weeks ago when someone close to my situation heard about it, looked me in the eye, and then said, "I believe you. It happened to me, too. Tell me more." At that moment I realized that simply being *believed* by someone affirms that you are not crazy. It hands back to the abused person their dignity, their worth, and the knowledge that they can indeed trust their perception of reality.

> This is a priceless gift we can give to others: "I believe you. I am so sorry you are experiencing this. Tell me more." Remember that I am going through this past year *knowing* what gaslighting is, how to recognize it, etc., and yet still it has taken a horrible toll. Yet still, in spite of my awareness of what I am experiencing,

I was stunned at the extraordinary healing power of that other person's simple "I believe you."

I have been asking myself ever since if I am giving to my friends, my loved ones, my students, etc., the gift of believing them. When people know you will believe them, they begin to realize they don't have to defend themselves, they don't have to "rehearse" in order to win the argument, they don't have to worry about presenting things in the most manipulative light so that they can persuade the person to believe them, etc. They can simply be themselves and express their truth, knowing that I do not need to be convinced of their rightness: just their story is enough. And I will believe them.

Too often, pastors hearing abused women confide their stories assume the woman is exaggerating, or simply speaking out of emotion. Especially given all the conditioning she has received in evangelicalism to accept "male headship" unquestioningly, with all of its trappings, it has probably taken extraordinary courage for her to come to the pastor at all. It is a slap in the face to be told to "avoid doing the things that make him angry" and to "focus on cooking his favorite meals."[50]

Early Intervention

The local church needs to intervene more decisively at the first sign of trouble or plea for help. They often don't. Since beginning research and hearing from other women in destructive marriages, I have learned that it is often the young, recent seminary graduates who are more prone to addressing serious marriage issues with a heavy-handed approach. Whereas older pastors with upwards of 30 years of experience witnessing marriage difficulties often counsel caution and are loathe to rush women into reconciliation, their younger (and less-experienced) counterparts tend to think that their one-size-fits-all model and proof-texts learned in seminary will provide formulaic solutions to every marriage difficulty – even abuse.

It is just not that simple.

What pastors need to do is protect women, not just by grudgingly allowing for physical "separation for a time," but by confronting the abuser's tactics head-on. Extremely intelligent and often crafty at the manipulation game, abusive men seem believable when they adopt the conciliatory "Christian" tone with the pastor, and explain how emotional and "unsubmissive" their

---

[50]   Actual advice to an abused woman from a 'biblical counseling' website.

wives are. Inexperienced pastors, pre-disposed to believe the man's side, often do nothing to help the woman – instead, they often side against her along with her husband. Controlling men enjoy this power-mongering to no end, and will often egg the woman on, with taunts that she "has a problem with authority" and "one day will answer to God for [her] sins." In actuality, of course, just the reverse is true – *they* one day will answer to God for how they have mistreated their wives – but abusive men are experts at turning black into white. Until more pastors become aware of this, and are trained at understanding the psychological makeup of abusive individuals (and the idols that drive them), nothing will change.

Providing Practical Help

A number of women who have come out of abusive marriages cite the difficulties that arose when they suddenly found themselves single mothers, especially without the support of family. Unable to pay rent, provide basic necessities for their children or themselves, they are often forced to turn to the state welfare available to them or rely on local charities. Many churches have an income from tithes and offerings well in surplus of their operating budget, and give liberally to overseas missions and local ministries. Helping the marginalized women in their own congregations who have had to flee abusive situations should be a priority, but rarely is it. These women often find themselves on the fringes of church society, and are surviving hand-to-mouth. For their local church to embrace them and provide practical things such as groceries, babysitting, and gas cards would be an enormous blessing to them. A huge ministry opportunity exists within the local churches' own sanctuaries.

Some para-church ministries such as Give Her Wings have stood in the gap, although due to the limitations of being completely donor-funded, Give Her Wings strictly vets women who may receive help. Women are ineligible if they are receiving any kind of state support, assistance from their families, or church aid. It is a sad testimony to the Church that most of them are not being aided in any way.

As mentioned earlier, more and more Christian ministries and churches are beginning to stand up and confront the problem of marital abuse head-on, although there is a long way to go towards unmasking and preventing the problem. The Baptist Churches of NSW & ACT have provided a free guide directed at training pastors in ending domestic abuse which may be downloaded through their website: http://nswactbaptists.org.au/wp-content/uploads/sites/19/2016/10/Domestic-Violence-Guide-for-Churches.pdf Their goal is to contribute to change in at least four areas:

- Prevention in our churches
- Prevention in our communities
- Provision of safe spaces for victims
- Rehabilitation for perpetrators

More Balanced Pre-Marital and Marriage Counseling

Many churches (even without a formal nouthetic counseling model) now do offer pre-marital counseling. This is a very helpful start for couples to learn a biblical model of marriage before their nuptials, and can no doubt assist them in identifying potential relationship problems before they appear. However, as counseling is offered overwhelmingly in complementarian churches, care must be taken to present a truly accurate picture of a Christ-like marriage. Over-emphasizing female "submission" to the expense of the husband's responsibility to love, honor and respect his wife as an equal partner leads to an attitude of entitlement, which can easily lead to abusive speech and behaviors as we have seen throughout this book. An emphasis on what it means to *honor* his wife as a co-laborer for the Gospel (albeit with different strengths and abilities than his) and on encouraging her to develop and use her gifts, rather than restricting or forbidding her, should be a requisite part of any pre-marital counseling program.

Furthermore, communication and the importance of affection in marriage should be acknowledged in the counseling room. While nouthetic counselors are trained to drill the "love is not a feeling; it is a choice" mantra into their counselees' heads, they often give the impression that marriage is a dry, emotionless obligatory relationship which is undertaken out of a sense of duty. Feelings of loneliness and isolation (let alone outright abuse) are often dismissed as unimportant, but the intimacy of the one-flesh union portrayed in Scripture paints a very different picture. Lack of communication and feeling de-valued as a human being, friend and partner are common traps in marriages that should not be minimized. Rather, they should be candidly addressed in the context of the counseling room before the couple enters into the marriage covenant. An excellent resource on this subject is *Starved for Affection*, by Focus on the Family's Dr. Randy Carlson. Where an imbalance of power is allowed to exist in marriage, or, worse yet, justified by a church, the soil is fertile for an abusive relationship to take hold.

Although abuse is not an issue appropriate to be addressed in couples counseling (it is not a marriage issue *per se*, but rather a unilateral sin of one party in the marriage), it is often treated as such by nouthetic counselors. Because of the stigma of abuse, false guilt that her "sin" may be partly responsible for her treatment, and fear she will not be believed, it is already difficult for women to seek out counseling within the church for any form of mistreatment. Once she takes this step, how the counselor then proceeds becomes critically important. Whether as part of marriage counseling, or individually meeting with the husband, some questions which need to be honestly considered include:

- How is the abuse evaluated?
- Is the woman believed?
- Is the counselor willing to confront the husband, or does he merely intend to get his "perspective on the marriage problems"?
- Does the abuser even admit to his behavior?
- Does he call his behavior "abuse," or does he attempt to minimize it by giving it other terms?
- Is he willing to change, and if so, how?
- Can he identify the destructive and sinful attitudes he holds toward his wife, and perhaps women in general?
- What form will ongoing (long-term) counseling take? How will progress towards repentance of abusive attitudes/behaviors be evaluated objectively, and by whom?
- If the couple is separated due to either physical or emotional abuse, is the counselor putting any pressure/time-frames or ultimatums on the victim for 'reconciliation'?
- What is the church's plan for gauging repentance, and how can they be sure the abusive individual is not 'playing the game' of counseling, with the purpose of getting his victim back (but with no real heart-change)?
- Are both parties willing and desirous of counseling (and/or reconciliation), or is coercion (including veiled threats of church discipline) being employed against the victim?

The last question is particularly relevant, as more churches tend to use the Matthew 18 process against the victim, without adequately addressing the abuser's sin or likelihood to change. These churches need not only to stop their witch-hunts of women fleeing abusive husbands, but need to provide a much more thorough and non-gender biased platform for counseling long before marriages start to unravel. Misogyny, no matter how skillfully it is cloaked in spiritual-sounding language, will always lead to abuse. Daughters of the King need to know they are safe, and have access to just treatment from those claiming to act with His authority.

Recognizing the Importance of Culture

Another way in which church leaders can take a proactive role in understanding the types of abuse that occur in Christian homes is by realizing we live in a multi-cultural society, and attempting to understand the way certain cultural mores and ways of thinking influence the male-female relationship within marriage. While it is tempting to believe that once someone becomes a Christian, his mind is completely renewed in Christ and cultural factors no longer influence him, many different ethnic communities can attest that this is not necessarily the case. Old ways of thinking and cultural conditioning can die hard, especially in sub-cultures where women are traditionally seen as inferior to men. In authoritarian churches, men from these cultural backgrounds can all too easily find spiritual justification for their misogyny by twisting key passages of Scripture to suit their needs. Pastors need to recognize this and be on guard.

In September 2016, The Biblical Counseling Coalition published an article I wrote after attending a two-day Slavic Christian women's conference in Connecticut and doing subsequent research on the epidemic of abuse and violence in the Slavic-American evangelical community. Very well received by women around the country (not just Slavic-American ladies), the article, "The Culture of Abuse in Christian Slavic Marriages" presented the problem of abuse being hidden or explained away through the eyes of women who had observed it first-hand.[51] While by no means unique or limited merely to Eastern European culture, Russian and Ukrainian evangelical women openly shared what their fears and frustrations were with pastors who simply don't understand how ingrained the misogynistic attitude is in their communities.

Although I never mentioned my former husband or church in the article, or even his (Slavic) country of origin, many of the women's observations and testimonies sounded so familiar to me that I took comfort in knowing I was not alone. My former husband was from Bulgaria, where we met and married, and blamed much of his treatment of me and the children on his ethnic background. Insofar as patterns of behavior that are considered socially acceptable in Eastern Europe, he was partially right – but I would counter: when one has the indwelling power of the Holy Spirit, *one's ethnic background or upbringing cannot be used as an excuse for sin.* In fact, in a biblical counseling session when we attempted to address his anger problem in 2014, my then-husband apologetically said to the pastor, "Eh, I'm Bulgarian...what can you do?" The counseling pastor countered humorously with, "And I'm from a big Italian family where everybody yells

---

[51] https://biblicalcounselingcoalition.org/2016/09/30/the-culture-of-abuse-in-christian-slavic-marriages/

at each other, but that doesn't make the Word of God any less true! Think of it...you could be the first Bulgarian who *doesn't sin*!"

While we all laughed at the time, holdover cultural conditioning and attitudes towards women should not be glossed over or dismissed lightly. It is very hard to undo unconscious beliefs held from childhood, especially when the abuser has seen humiliating treatment of women (his mother; sisters; aunts) modeled before him all his life. Since I work as a medical interpreter in several different hospitals, I have had the opportunity to get to know other linguists from many nations and backgrounds who have made similar observations.

Shiraz, a middle-aged interpreter originally from Iran, told me about one of her male patients who habitually criticizes and demeans his wife in front of hospital staff. "One day, he said in front of the doctor how the world would be freer and our lives more blessed without the stench of women, while looking at his wife," she said. "The doctor didn't react, but said 'Your wife is such a beautiful rose; surely you know how blessed you are!' He has been in America 35 years, but he still does not understand that women are not property. The look of shame in [his wife's] eyes, as she lowered her head, tells me that this is something she endures every day."

Notwithstanding this problem, we must be careful not to over-estimate the role of culture in an abusive spouse. It should never be used as an excuse for mistreatment. In countries like Albania, where domestic abuse is a significant problem, evangelical pastors do counsel biblically, but take a much more realistic view about the likelihood of reconciliation. Many of them have witnessed their own sisters and mothers being abused, and realize how hard the controlling and abusive mindset is to turn around. And yet, abuse is still recognizable (as it is everywhere) as being distinct from paternalism.

Following my divorce, a young woman half my age said to me, "Marie, I am sorry to hear about your situation. I noticed when your family was here... your husband seemed like a very strict, unyielding guy. I wouldn't have thought much of it, but before that, when we were talking on Facebook, I noticed you always had to ask his permission for everything. When you were here with your family...well, we all saw that you were in a very unhealthy situation. And we were all worried about you, honestly. This is something not normal...not even for Albania."

While recognizing that cultural mores may lie at least partially behind abusive attitudes and behaviors, this should never be used as an excuse to justify or "explain it away." Even within cultures generally considered to be "patriarchal," (as seen in the examples above), discerning individuals are able to spot the difference between traditional attitudes and behavior and words that are truly destructive and hurtful. With the full counsel of God and the guidance of the Holy Spirit to guide them, how much more should Christian church leaders be able to discern this sin?

The Importance of Integration in the Church

Insisting on separate Bible studies and fellowship groups for men and women can also add to the invisible barriers and give credence to the superior/inferior standing. Gender segregation of this type is an unbiblical concept, and does nothing to promote mutual respect and spiritual growth together. In Acts 20 and elsewhere in the New Testament, including the Gospels, we see men and women learning, teaching and serving side by side.

Not only is this separation artificial and unnecessary in the modern church, it can be detrimental to the women who want a deeper, exegetical study of Scripture. I have noticed consistently that while men's Bible studies tend to be doctrinally rich and written by respected theologians, what we women are offered tends to be more subjective, feelings-based teaching; often written by women with no seminary training or credentials whatsoever. Unless we take the initiative to study commentaries and the deeper doctrinal books on our own, there is not much "meat" typically offered to women in church-led Bible studies. Whether by design or by default, keeping us segregated into our own "ladies' Bible studies" does not do much to train us in a correct division of the Word (2 Timothy 2:15). Hermeneutics is a process in which everyone should engage. By having equal opportunity to study the Word of God together, it is less likely that some in the congregation will be able to cherry-pick certain passages to wield as weapons over others.

Ashley Easter, an egalitarian Christian blogger, writes about what she calls "the infantilization of women in the Church":

> I believe "benevolent" patriarchy is a form of infantilization. It reduces women to an infant or childlike state by suggesting they are in need of the more mature, "adult" authority of a man in their life. Where benevolent patriarchy is practiced, women are not encouraged or trusted to become fully mature, independent adults. They are not allowed to be fully in charge of their own destinies or given equally-weighted input in marriage relationships.

> I have seen women stunted or delayed in their maturation by forced naivety, lack of practical education, and limited opportunities. The infantilization of women becomes a self-

fulfilling prophecy. Because women are believed to lack personal maturity and deciding power, they are denied opportunities to mature into these functions, thus creating a confirmation bias scenario.[52]

Of course, patriarchy, even "benevolent" patriarchy, is not the classical complementarian position or practice. While the former demeans women (or "infantilizes" them, as Ashley puts it), the latter simply limits the church offices women may hold without diminishing them to second-class status. It is the patriarchal bias she is speaking against, as am I, which leads to disrespect and (taken to its logical conclusion) abuse. Naturally, no patriarchal church would want to label itself "authoritarian," and so "benevolent patriarchy" becomes a condescending curtain behind which sanctified misogyny can hide. However, the term is an oxymoron. "Benevolent patriarchy" can no more exist than a "benevolent dictatorship" can.

Serving together (whether in missions-related work or intra-church activity) is also an important part of church life, and should not be limited to "ladies-only" or "men-only" ministry opportunities. Where believers serve together, mutual respect flourishes as each is individually encouraged to use his or her gifts. There are many opportunities to get involved both in local church and para-church ministries that do not involve congregational preaching, so the complementarian stance, rightly understood, shouldn't become an issue. Even the most hardline complementarian cannot find a Bible verse to prevent women from organizing a Youth Camp activity, making budgetary decisions on a missions committee, or negotiating a mortgage for the church's real estate company. To suggest otherwise is to promote one's own agenda – not Christ's.

Preaching Against Abuse

Different forms of domestic abuse, verbal/emotional abuse of wives by their husbands in particular, is often glossed over or ignored at conservative churches and the conferences they endorse. "Unedifying speech," when mentioned in sermons, is usually limited to gossip and swearing – rarely is it applied to the man who consistently tears his wife down with sarcasm, criticism, and intimidation. While this by no means indicates that pastors advocate or encourage contemptuous treatment of women, the men in their congregations with anger and/or control issues or narcissistic tendencies "hear" justification for their attitudes in the patriarchal message of "Men lead; women submit." The issue of contention in the family and outright abuse needs to be tackled

---

[52] http://www.ashleyeaster.com/blog/infantilization-of-women

head-on and recognized for the sin that it is. Many pastors are already speaking out against this twisting of Scripture, but not nearly enough. Jeff Crippin has over a dozen sermons on the subject available as podcasts on Sermon Audio. Sam Powell is another (Reformed) pastor who has had the courage to preach and write against abuses rampant in the Church. Moody Church Media also has webcasts devoted to healing from abuse, and what marriage is (and isn't) available through their website (www.moodymedia.org).

The excessive teaching on "male headship" in Reformed churches, in particular, needs to be balanced by more practical instruction in loving one's wife as Christ loves the Church. Sermon series on Deuteronomy 6 and Ephesians 5:22 need to be tempered with clear teaching from the pulpit and in men's Bible studies on 1 Peter 3:7 and Ephesians 5:25. The clarity of Galatians 3:28 on the equal standing of the sexes before God should negate any rationalization of misogyny within the Church. Far from denying the God-given differences and gifts of men and women, this passage and others like it demonstrate that there is no biblical precedent for men to use their power to subdue their wives.

Writer Valerie Jacobsen has this to say about the dichotomy of normal trials in the Christian life, and the abuses of power inflicted upon women under the false guise of "complementarianism":

> There is a very odd inconsistency in how patriarchy and suffering are viewed. On the one hand, people say that if it's biblical patriarchy and hierarchy, then it's really quite lovely all the time. (The only real patriarchy is "nice" patriarchy.) If anyone suffered under something called by these names, well, the victims weren't too swift and were obviously not doing it right. It's no reflection on the doctrines!
>
> On the other hand, just about every book written for wives on how to live in biblical patriarchy and hierarchy has addressed the issue of grave suffering and has considered it an unavoidable (and in some senses, desirable) aspect of the system. Women are taught how to look at that suffering, what to do about it, and what they should hope to see from it.
>
> Desirable, in that a wife's suffering (they never mention the suffering children) and her efforts to perfect her own submission can help her husband obtain salvation. (We either go to 1 Peter 3:1 believing Ephesians 2:8-10 and knowing that salvation is by grace, or we don't.)[53]

---

[53] Quoted from www.Facebook.com. Used with permission of the writer.

Many pastors earnestly desire to save and reconcile broken marriages, but they fail to see what is often the root problem: *abuse*, rooted in *an unbiblical imbalance of power*. Throughout Proverbs and elsewhere, we see that God clearly judges the abuse of power. He does not justify it, nor commend the men for being "spiritual leaders" or true "patriarchs." Much pain and many broken marriages would be avoided if a message of mutual respect and understanding were preached, with practical consideration given on how to "show honor to the woman." Addressing these fundamental relational issues should be an integral part of seminary training, as pastors will expect to be shepherding families.

Lastly, the teaching that abuse is "never biblical grounds for divorce" seems to be proliferating especially among younger pastors who have graduated from seminaries such as Southeastern Baptist Theological Seminary (SEBT) and Dallas Theological Seminary. More attention needs to be focused at the seminary level on the complexity of different types of marital conflict and abuse, as well as the full counsel of Scripture on abuse of power and God's view of oppression (as well as the provisions of the Mosaic marriage covenant and Pauline abandonment clause). The absolutist view against divorce (and re-marriage) in almost all cases promoted by many popular Neo-Calvinist leaders, such as John Piper and John MacArthur, is harmful to women and reveals a telescopic reading of Scripture. Worse, employing "church discipline" as a punitive measure against women who flee their abusers is a perversion of the restorative intent of Matthew 18. There is a serious need for remedial teaching in some of the nation's best seminaries when it comes to the more unpleasant sides of marriage.

A High View of Marriage

A "high view of marriage" means teaching Christian families what it means to keep covenant with one another in the privacy of our homes where God sees all things. It means preaching against covenant-breaking evil and treachery. It means getting down in the trenches to help us build holy, healthy, safe families by whatever means necessary, including lawful divorce when needed.

A "high view of God's sovereignty" means teaching us to submit our hearts to God's providence – to what is actually happening in our lives – and not pressuring us to form our responses on a presumption that whatever good we could wish will certainly come to pass, in time. A high view of God's sovereignty means that we will encourage one another to accept that life is not always safe and that we will not always get whatever we want if we will only pray hard enough and wait long enough (James 4:13-17).

A high view of marriage isn't a perfectionistic obsession with the church's divorce statistics, with the moments of adjudication in court, or with the paperwork that lawful divorce requires. This would be like admiring the birth certificate, but refusing to kiss the baby! And yet this is what many teachers have done. They have claimed a "high view of marriage" while they have reserved their first allegiance for covenant-breaking.

And where the innocent spouse has been a woman, they have often been especially complacent toward our suffering! They have pressured us to believe that if we would endure more covenant-breaking evil for more years, we could trade our ongoing agony for a higher level of sanctification for ourselves and a greater chance at salvation for our husbands! (These are false doctrines.) [54]

Christian leaders, take heed. Please do not patronizingly thank us "for sharing our hearts" when we come to you with serious problems. Stop telling women that they can end abuse by submitting to their abuser or affirming his leadership more strongly. Stop believing the abuser's heavily-twisted version of the story. Above all, stop treating the spouse who exposes the abuse and evil in the household as the villain, or the "real abuser."

Come to us in the trenches.

Listen to us. Believe us. Be willing to admit that abuse is real; it is evil; and, barring a miracle of God, it may never change. Have enough humility to admit you do not possess all the answers to abused women's trials, even if you hold a seminary degree. Be ready to learn that the permanence view of marriage you hold to does not hold up in all situations, where the marriage covenant has been destroyed by sin. Be aware that not all who are confronted will repent, at least not in the biblical sense of the word. Acknowledge that the abused Christian women has a scarred, wounded soul and needs compassionate counsel to restore her trust in God as her loving Father.

Above all, be ready, willing and able to listen to the women in your congregations, and treat them with the loving compassion that Jesus does. Only when you lead by example will the Church really have made inroads against the insidious evil of marital abuse – an evil that is hidden in plain sight.

---

[54]   IBID.

Recommended Resources for Healing from Emotional and Spiritual Abuse

Books:

Who's Pushing Your Buttons: Handling the Difficult People in Your Life by John Townsend (Thomas Nelson)

The Emotionally Destructive Marriage by Leslie Vernick (WaterBrook)

Foolproofing Your Life: How to Effectively Deal with the Impossible People in Your Life by Jan Silvious (WaterBrook)

The Verbally Abusive Relationship by Patricia Evans (Adams Media)

Healing from Hidden Abuse by Shannon Thomas, LCSW (MAST Publishing House)

Why Does He Do That? by Lundy Bancroft (Berkley Books)

A Cry for Justice: How the Evil of Domestic Abuse Hides in Your Church by Jeff Crippen (Calvary Press)

Unholy Charade: Unmasking the Domestic Abuser in the Church by Jeff Crippen and Rebecca Davis (Justice Keepers Publishing)

Safe People by Henry Cloud and John Townsend (Zondervan)

In Sheep's Clothing: Understanding and Dealing with Manipulative People by George Simon Jr., Phd. (Parkhurst Brothers Publishers Inc.)

Online Ministries/Blogs:

Give Her Wings – giveherwings.com

A Cry for Justice – cryingoutforjustice.com

Self-Care Haven – selfcarehaven.wordpress.com

The Spiritual Abuse Survivor Blog Network – patheos.com/blogs/nolongerquivering/spiritual-abuse-survivor-blogs-network/

Spiritual Sounding Board – spiritualsoundingboard.com

Hagar's Sisters – hagarssisters.org

Visionary Womanhood – emotionalabusesurvivor.com